Fodor's 94 Pocket Paris

Reprinted from *Fodor's Paris '94*

Fodor's Travel Publications, Inc.
New York • Toronto • London •
Sydney • Auckland

Fodor's Pocket Paris

Editors: Suzanne De Galan and Katherine Kane
Editorial Contributors: David Downie, Corinne LaBalme, Robert Noah, Alex Siegel
Creative Director: Fabrizio La Rocca
Cartographer: David Lindroth
Illustrator: Karl Tanner
Cover Photograph: Catherine Karnow

Design: Vignelli Associates

Contents

Maps and Plans

Foreword

While every care has been taken to ensure the accuracy of the information in this guide, the passage of time will always bring change, and consequently, the publisher cannot accept responsibility for errors that may occur.

All prices and opening times quoted here are based on information supplied to us at press time. Hours and admission fees may change, however, and the prudent traveler will avoid inconvenience by calling ahead.

Fodor's wants to hear about your travel experiences, both pleasant and unpleasant. When a hotel or restaurant fails to live up to its billing, let us know and we will investigate the complaint and revise our entries where the facts warrant it.

Send your letters to the editors of Fodor's Travel Publications, 201 East 50th Street, New York, NY 10022.

Paris

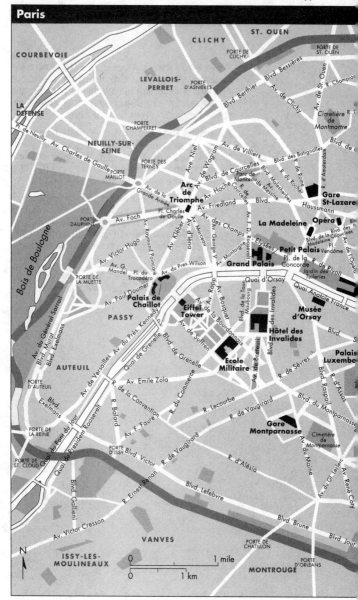

ST. OUEN

CLICHY

COURBEVOIE

PORTE DE
CLICHY

PORTE DE
ST. OUEN

LEVALLOIS-
PERRET

PORTE
D'ASNIÈRES

Blvd. Berthier

Blvd. Bessières

Av. de Clichy

Av. de St. Ouen

R. Champ...

Cimetière
de
Montmartre

Blvd. de ...

LA
DÉFENSE

PORTE
CHAMPERRET

NEUILLY-SUR-
SEINE

Pt. de Neuilly

Av. Charles de Gaulle

PORTE MAILLOT

PORTE DES
TERNES

Av. de Villiers

Av. Niel

Av. de Wagram

Blvd. de Courcelles

Gare de
Monceau

Blvd. Malesherbes

Blvd. de Rome

Blvd. des Batignolles

Blvd. d'Amsterdam

Gare
St-Lazare

Arc
de
Triomphe

Av. de la
Grande Armée

Av. Hoche

Av. de Messine

Av. Friedland

Blvd. Haussmann

La Madeleine

Opéra

PORTE
DAUPHINE

Av. Foch

Pl. Charles
de Gaulle

Av. des Champs

Élysées

Blvd. de la Madeleine

Blvd. des C...

Bois de Boulogne

Av. Victor Hugo

Av. Kléber

Av. d'Iéna

Av. George V

Av. Marceau

Av. Montaigne

Av. F. D. Roosevelt

Petit Palais

Grand Palais

Pl. de la
Concorde

Blvd. de la Capucines

Pl.
Vendôme

Jardin des
Tuileries

R. de Rivoli

PORTE DE
LA MUETTE

Av. Raymond Poincaré

Av. G.
Mandel

Pl. du
Trocadéro

Av. du Prés. Wilson

Palais de
Chaillot

Av. Paul Doumer

Quai d'Orsay

Musée
d'Orsay

Quai Anatole France

PASSY

Eiffel
Tower

Av. Rapp

Av. de la Tour Maubourg

Av. de la
Bourdonnais

Av. de Suffren

Hôtel des
Invalides

des Invalides

Blvd.

AUTEUIL

Av. du Prés. Kennedy

Quai de Grenelle

Blvd. de Grenelle

Av. de la Motte

Ecole
Militaire

Av. de Breteuil

R. de Sèvres

Palais
Luxembo...

Blvd. Raspail

R. d'Assas

PORTE
D'AUTEUIL

Blvd.
Exelmans

Av. de Versailles

R. de la Convention

R. Balard

Av. Emile Zola

R. du Commerce

R. Lecourbe

R. de Vaugirard

Blvd. du Montparnasse

Av. du Général Sarrail

Blvd. Murat

Blvd. Exelmans

Quai du Pont du Jour

Quai du Président Roosevelt

Av. F. Faure

Blvd. Victor

R. de Vaugirard

Gare
Montparnasse

Cimetière
de
Montparnasse

Av. du Maine

PORTE DE
LA REINE

PORTE
D'ISSY

R. d'Alésia

Av. du Gl Leclerc

Av. René Coty

PORTE DE
ST. CLOUD

Blvd. Galliéni

Blvd. Lefebvre

Blvd. Brune

Blvd. Jour...

Av. Victor Cresson

VANVES

PORTE DE
CHATILLON

PORTE
D'ORLEANS

ISSY-LES-
MOULINEAUX

MONTROUGE

R. Ernest Renan

N

0   1 mile

0   1 km

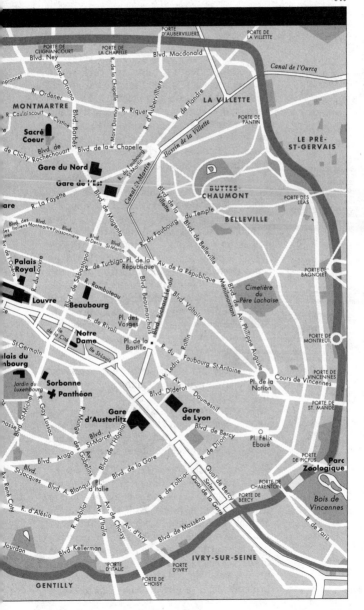

Introduction

By John G. Morris

John G. Morris has worked as a journalist for major American newspapers and magazines—the Washington Post, The New York Times, Life, Ladies' Home Journal, *and* National Geographic. *He now contributes regularly to the* International Herald Tribune.

You have heard it said that "Paris would be great if it weren't for the Parisians." If a Frenchman says it, it means that he is determined to be provincial. But if it comes from a foreigner, it probably means that he or she has had an unfortunate linguistic encounter. It takes a certain nerve to try out one's French, no matter one's level. A former *New York Times* Paris bureau chief told me he got by only because his French was "audacious." Many foreigners, and I am one, are afraid of being laughed at. The cure for this is to make a faux pas so ridiculous that you can tell it on yourself. A young photographer friend of mine, for example, was trying to tell some French friends about his first date with a girl of good family and prim reputation. He thought he was telling them that he had kissed her good night—the polite peck. Instead, he was saying that he had bedded her the first night. They were impressed but incredulous.

Paris is the city where, once you are known, shopkeepers greet you coming and going and proprietors shake your hand as you leave their restaurants. It is the city where bus drivers may reopen the door for you if you come on the run, and where bellmen are sometimes too proud to linger for a tip.

Not that Parisians are perfect. There are the usual shady characters who populate our urbanized world. There are pickpockets, just to make you feel at home. *En garde!* Weapons are not often used in Paris crime, but thieves can be ingenious. A friend from Manhattan was the victim of a classic ploy. Sensing that his wallet had been lifted while he was standing in awe of Notre Dame, he whirled on the probable thief, a girl of about 12. To attest her innocence, she lifted her dress, revealing a totally naked body. Our friend was too flustered to pursue the matter further.

Paris is not France, but France would be unimaginable without Paris. Here, past and present coexist, sometimes comfortably, sometimes uneasily. Children play house in the playground of the Cluny museum, on the spot where Romans took their leisure in baths 100 meters long.

Called Lutetia by the Romans but renamed for the Parisii, a Celtic tribe, Paris has been a settlement on the Seine for more than two millennia. Blood has flowed here as constantly as the river. Crossing the place de la Concorde, one still shivers at the thought of the 1,344 persons beheaded there by the guillotine, including King Louis XVI and Marie Antoinette. Tourists flock to the Sacré-Coeur, at once the ugliest and boldest church in Paris. It stands on a hill named Montmartre, for the Christian martyrs; one of them, Saint Denis, is said to have carried his severed head in his hands as he walked north out of the city in the third century. Joan of Arc was wounded in Paris in 1429, but it was another woman, Geneviève, a shepherdess from Nanterre, who became the special saint of Paris, having rallied the city against Attila the Hun. Today, students at the Sorbonne study in a reading room as long as a football field and high enough for a dropkick, in the library of her name. A department store, La Samaritaine, backs up against the church of St-Germain l'Auxerrois, from whose tower bells rang on the night of August 24, 1572, to signal the prearranged massacre of 3,000 Huguenots. A short walk away, at a Jewish restaurant called Goldenberg's in the heart of the Marais district, a mini-massacre, on August 9, 1982, took the lives of six people at lunchtime.

Only London and Rome can even come close to holding such treasures of the past as does Paris. Hitler, furious with the retreat of his forces in World War II, ordered the city burned, but his own commander failed him and Allied forces swept in. To sense the grandeur that would have been lost, try sitting on a bench above the Seine on the pedestrian Pont des Arts, which offers a kind of gracious scaffolding over the river. Face downstream and set your watch by the clock of the Institut Français on the Left Bank as the rays of the sun, setting into the muddy green river, gild the towers of the Louvre on your right. Or look upstream at the Pont Neuf as it crosses the prow of the Ile de la Cité. Beyond but out of sight is the Ile St-Louis, perhaps the world's most perfect village, standing almost exactly as it began—a real estate development built on pastures of the 17th century.

Paris has a museum for every period and taste. Parisians argue museums as Americans fight over baseball teams. They tend either to loathe or love the Beaubourg, its red and blue insides exposed like an oil refinery. The exciting Musée d'Orsay is dedicated to the art of the period 1848–1914 and houses the great collection of Impressionists that was formerly in the Jeu de Paume.

I first entered the Louvre in 1944, only to find it virtually empty. The foresighted French had evacuated and hidden most of the great masterpieces at the onset of war. All that remained of the *Mona Lisa* was a chalk scrawl to indicate its normal hanging place. Nevertheless, the Grande Galérie of the Louvre was just as staggering a spectacle as it is today. The Louvre is a palace so vast that one can make a fresh discovery on every visit.

Great exhibitions are not limited to museums. The Grand Palais, a marvel of turn-of-the-century iron and glass construction, and its little neighbor of the same vintage, the Petit Palais, occasionally attract lines that stretch far down avenue Winston Churchill. As if those are not enough, the city has built another huge complex, a kind of fairground of halls, playgrounds, and theaters (one of which is enclosed in a shining sphere) on the site of the former slaughter-houses of La Villette, on the city's outskirts.

There are another dozen or so art museums. The Musée Guimet has Oriental art; the Marmottan is a mansion containing Monets and others. Museums have been created in the studios of Rodin, Delacroix, and Brancusi. Paris has major museums of anthropology, natural history, history, and science, and smaller ones dealing with everything from advertising and bread to urban transport and wine. The Musée Grévin, the waxworks museum on the boulevard Montmartre and in the Forum des Halles, is perhaps the most amusing of all.

If you're a nosy type, one who loves to poke and peek, a certain amount of respectful audacity will take you far in Paris. Instead of taking the guided tour at the Bourse, or stock exchange, you can try to talk your way into a look at the trading floor. Nearby, at the Bibliothèque Nationale, without a reader's card, you can look into the main reading room or the equally impressive periodicals room. For lawyers, a place of interest is the Palais de Justice, with courtrooms where black-robed judges and *avocats* hear and plead cases all day long. Just walking the halls there is a spectacle; one can tiptoe into courts in session. In the waiting rooms of the nearby Préfecture de Police, you will find scenes of poverty and desperation reminiscent of Daumier.

Notre Dame is just a bit farther; for your first visit, try entering through the north portal instead of through the nave, as most tourists do. You will then immediately confront the most glorious of the three rose windows. Stay for a mass or an organ concert.

S ome come to Paris just to eat. They come laden with research, with starred lists, credit cards, and calculated appetites. Many have done their homework well, with one or more of the useful books that devote themselves to mouth-watering descriptions of Parisian delicacies. My own approach is more casual; to my way of thinking, it's rather difficult to get a *bad* meal in Paris.

The sheer profusion of places to eat in Paris is staggering. There are, for example, 12,000 places where one can get a cup of tea or coffee—*or* a glass of wine or beer—a convenience that is one of the finer attributes of French civilization. I go sometimes by hearsay, sometimes by looks, often by ambience. The *carte* posted at the door offers further clues, especially as to price. The same rules apply in Paris as elsewhere: One tends to pay for name and fame. Some places seem so cheap that one gets suspicious, but there is often more fun in a bistro than in an elegant two-star.

Next to dining, entertainment is the most appealing industry of Paris. The week begins on Wednesday with the appearance of *Pariscope,* one of the three weekly bibles for those who go out often. A typical issue will list the 300 films that play the 384 cinemas in Paris and environs in an average week. That total includes 98 revivals, but not the films playing in the 14 film festivals or the 43 films screened free at the film libraries of the subsidized Beaubourg and Palais de Chaillot, or the 23 "special screenings" of various kinds.

In this same typical week, there are 18 works being performed in the 10 publicly supported theaters (Comédie Française, the Opéra, etc.). Another 101 theatrical pieces are being performed on 76 commercial stages, including works by Shakespeare, Strindberg, Brecht, Aristophanes, Chekhov, Sartre, Neil Simon, and Sam Shepard—most, but not all, in French. Another 160 cafés, cabarets, music halls, discos, and nightclubs offer programs ranging from political satire to striptease, New Orleans jazz, and the traditional cancan. Churches often offer chamber music. In this typical week, 96 concerts and 13 ballets are performed.

Paris is the home of the exile. It is here that Chopin came to compose, Picasso to paint, Joyce to write *Ulysses*. In Paris, even more than in London and New York, it is possible to live as a citizen of the world. It is almost possible to forget one's race, one's religion, almost possible to believe all men are brothers. Burnoose and sari, blue jeans and haute couture walk side by side. Gallic cynicism and *la vie en rose* go together. Victor Hugo aptly stated the message of Paris:

Cities are bibles of stone. This city possesses no single dome, roof, or pavement that does not convey some message of alliance and of union, and that does not offer some lesson, example, or advice. Let the people of all the world come to this prodigious alphabet of monuments, of tombs, and of trophies to learn peace and to unlearn the meaning of hatred. Let them be confident. For Paris has proven itself. To have once been Lutèce and to have become Paris—what could be a more magnificent symbol! To have been mud and to have become spirit!

1 Essential Information

Before You Go

Government Tourist Offices

Contact the French Government Tourist Office for free information.

In the United States 610 5th Ave., New York, NY 10020, tel. 212/315–0888 or 212/757–1125; 645 N. Michigan Ave., Chicago, IL 60611, tel. 312/337–6301; 2305 Cedar Springs Rd., Dallas, TX 75201, tel. 214/720–4010; 9401 Wilshire Blvd., Beverly Hills, CA 90212, tel. 213/271–6665; 1 Hallidie Plaza, Suite 250, San Francisco, CA 94102, tel. 415/986–4174.

In Canada 1981 McGill College Ave., Suite 490, Montreal, Quebec H3A 2W9, tel. 514/288–4264; 1 Dundas St. W, Suite 2405, Box 8, Toronto, Ontario M5G 1Z3, tel. 416/593–4723.

In the United Kingdom 178 Piccadilly, London W1V 0AL, tel. 071/629–1272.

When to Go

The major tourist season in France stretches from Easter to mid-September, but Paris has much to offer at every season. Paris in the early spring can be disappointingly damp; June is delightful, with good weather and plenty of cultural and other attractions. July and August can be sultry and dusty. Moreover, many restaurants, theaters, and small shops close for at least four weeks in summer.

September is ideal. Cultural life revives after the summer break and sunny weather often continues through the first half of October. The ballet and theater are in full swing in November, but the weather is part wet-and-cold, part bright-and-sunny.

December is dominated by the *fêtes de fin d'année* (end-of-year festivities), with splendid displays in food shops and restaurants and a busy theater, ballet, and opera season into January. February and March are the worst months, weatherwise, but with the coming of Easter, Paris starts looking beautiful again.

Climate What follow are the average daily maximum and minimum temperatures for Paris.

Jan.	43F	6C	May	68F	20C	Sept.	70F	21C
	34	1		49	10		53	12
Feb.	45F	7C	June	73F	23C	Oct.	60F	16C
	34	1		55	13		46	8
Mar.	54F	12C	July	76F	25C	Nov.	50F	10C
	39	4		58	14		40	5
Apr.	60F	16C	Aug.	75F	24C	Dec.	44F	7C
	43	6		58	14		36	2

Information Sources For current weather conditions for cities in the United States and abroad, plus the local time and helpful travel tips, call the **Weather Channel Connection** (tel. 900/WEATHER; 95¢ per minute) from a touch-tone phone.

National Holidays (1994) With 11 national holidays (*jours fériés*) and five weeks of paid vacation, the French have their share of repose. In May there is a holiday nearly every week, so be prepared for stores, banks, and museums to shut their doors for days at a time. Bastille Day (July 14) is observed in true French form, with an annual military parade down the Champs-Elysées and a fireworks display at the Eiffel Tower.

January 1 (New Year's Day); April 4 (Easter Monday); May 1 (Labor Day); May 8 (VE Day); May 12 (Ascension); May 23 (Pentecost Monday); July 14 (Bastille Day); August 15 (Assumption); November 1 (All Saints); November 11 (Armistice); December 25 (Christmas).

What to Pack

Clothing Pack light: Baggage carts are scarce at airports, and luggage restrictions on international flights are tight. What you pack depends more on the time of year than on any particular dress code. It can rain a fair amount in Paris, even in the summer, so consider bringing a raincoat and umbrella. Otherwise, pack as you would for a major American city: formal clothes for formal restaurants and nightclubs, casual clothes elsewhere. Jeans are as popular in Paris as anywhere and are perfectly acceptable for sightseeing and informal dining. However, a jeans-and-sneakers outfit will raise eyebrows at the theater, at expensive restaurants, and when visiting French families. Note that men and women wearing shorts will not be allowed in many churches and cathedrals.

Wear sturdy walking shoes for sightseeing: Paris is full of cobblestone streets, and many historic buildings are surrounded by gravel paths. To protect yourself against purse snatchers and pickpockets, take a handbag with long straps that you can sling across your body, bandolierstyle, with a zippered compartment for your money and passport—French law requires that you carry identification at all times.

Miscellaneous If you have a health problem that requires you to take a prescription drug, pack enough to last the duration of the trip or have your doctor write a prescription using the drug's generic name, as brand names vary widely from country to country. If you're staying in budget hotels, take along small bars of soap. And don't forget to pack a list of the addresses of offices that supply refunds for lost or stolen traveler's checks.

Luggage Free baggage allowances on an airline depend
Regulations on the airline, the route, and the class of your ticket. In general, on domestic flights and on international flights between the United States and foreign destinations, you are entitled to check two bags—neither exceeding 62 inches, or 158 centimeters (length + width + height), or weighing more than 70 pounds (32 kilograms). A third piece may be brought aboard as a carryon; its total dimensions are generally limited to less than 45 inches (114 centimeters), so it will fit easily under the seat in front of you or in the overhead compartment. There are variations, so ask in advance. The single rule, a Federal Aviation Administration safety regulation that pertains to carry-on baggage on U.S. airlines, requires only that carryons be properly stowed and allows the airline to limit allowances and tailor them to different aircraft and operational conditions. Charges for excess, oversize, or overweight pieces vary, so inquire before you pack.

If you are flying between two foreign destinations, note that baggage allowances may be determined not by the piece method but by the weight method, which generally allows 88 pounds (40 kilograms) of luggage in first class, 66 pounds (30 kilograms) in business class, and 44 pounds (20 kilograms) in economy. If your flight between two cities abroad *connects* with your transatlantic or transpacific flight, the piece method still applies.

Safeguarding Your Luggage Before leaving home, itemize your bags' contents and their worth; this list will help you estimate the extent of your loss if your bags go astray. To minimize that risk, tag them inside and out with your name, address, and phone number. (If you use your home address, cover it so that potential thieves can't see it.) At check-in, make sure that the tag attached by baggage handlers bears the correct three-letter code for your destination. If your bags do not arrive with you, or if you detect damage, do not leave the airport until you've filed a written report with the airline.

Electricity The electrical current in Paris is 220 volts, 50 cycles alternating current (AC); the United States runs on 110-volt, 60-cycle AC current. Unlike wall outlets in the United States, which accept plugs with two flat prongs, outlets in France take plugs with two round prongs.

Adapters, Converters, Transformers To plug in U.S.-made appliances abroad, you'll need an adapter plug. To reduce the voltage entering the appliance from 220 to 110 volts, you'll also need a converter, unless it is a dual-voltage appliance, made for travel. There are converters for high-wattage appliances (such as hair dryers), low-wattage items (such as electric toothbrushes and razors), and combination models. Hotels sometimes have outlets marked "For Shavers Only" near the sink; these are 110-volt outlets for low-wattage appliances; don't use them for a high-wattage appliance. If you're traveling with a laptop computer, especially an older one, you may need a transformer—a type of converter used with electronic-circuitry products. Newer laptop computers are auto-sensing, operating equally well on 110 and 220 volts (so you need only the appropriate adapter plug).

French Currency

The unit of currency in France is the franc, which is divided into 100 centimes. The bills are 500, 200, 100, and 50 francs. Coins are 20, 10, 5, 2, and 1 francs and 50, 20, 10, and 5 centimes. At press time (mid-1993), the exchange rate was 5.2 francs to the dollar and 8.5 francs to the pound.

Passports and Visas

If your passport is lost or stolen abroad, report it immediately to the nearest embassy or consulate and to the local police. If you can provide the consular officer with the information contained in the passport, he or she will usually be able to issue you a new passport. For this reason, it is a good idea to keep a copy of the data page of your passport in a separate place, or to leave the passport number, date, and place of issuance with a relative or friend at home.

U.S. Citizens All U.S. citizens, even infants, need a valid passport to enter France for stays of up to 90 days.

You can pick up new and renewal application forms at any of the 13 U.S. Passport Agency offices and at some post offices and courthouses. Although passports are usually mailed within two weeks of your application's receipt, it's best to allow three weeks for delivery in low season, five weeks or more from April through summer. Call the Department of State Office of Passport Services' information line (1425 K St. NW, Washington, DC 20522, tel. 202/647–0518) for details.

Canadian Canadian citizens need a valid passport to enter
Citizens France. Application forms are available at 23 regional passport offices as well as post offices and travel agencies. Whether applying for a first or subsequent passport, you must apply in person. Children under 16 may be included on a parent's passport but must have their own passport to travel alone. Passports are valid for five years and are usually mailed within two weeks of an application's receipt. For more information in

English or French, call the passport office (tel. 514/283–2152).

U.K. Citizens Citizens of the United Kingdom need a valid passport to enter France. Applications for new and renewal passports are available from main post offices as well as at the six passport offices, located in Belfast, Glasgow, Liverpool, London, Newport, and Peterborough. You may apply in person at all passport offices, or by mail to all except the London office. Children under 16 may travel on a parent's passport when accompanying them. All passports are valid for 10 years. Allow a month for processing.

A British Visitor's Passport is valid for holidays and some business trips of up to three months to France. It can include both partners of a married couple. A British visitor's passport is valid for one year and will be issued on the same day that you apply. You must apply in person at a main post office.

Customs and Duties

On Arrival If you're coming from a European Community (EC) country, you may import duty free: (1) 300 cigarettes or 150 cigarillos or 75 cigars or 400 grams of tobacco; (2) 5 liters of table wine and, in addition, (a) 1.5 liters of alcohol over 22% volume (most spirits) or (b) 3 liters of alcohol under 22% volume (fortified or sparkling wine) or (c) 3 more liters of table wine; (3) 90 milliliters of perfume and 375 milliliters of toilet water; and (4) other goods to the value of 2,000 francs (400 francs for those under 15).

If you're coming from anywhere else, you may import duty free: (1) 200 cigarettes or 100 cigarillos or 50 cigars or 250 grams of tobacco (twice that if you live outside of Europe); (2) 2 liters of wine and, in addition, (a) 1 liter of alcohol over 22% volume (most spirits) or (b) 2 liters of alcohol under 22% volume (fortified or sparkling wine) or (c) 2 more liters of table wine; (3) 60 milliliters of perfume and 250 milliliters of toilet water; and (4) other goods to the value of 2,400 francs (620 francs for those under 15).

Any amount of French or foreign currency may be brought into France, but foreign currencies converted into francs may be reconverted into a foreign currency only up to the equivalent of 5,000 francs.

Returning Home
U.S. Customs

Provided you've been out of the country for at least 48 hours and haven't already used the exemption, or any part of it, in the past 30 days, you may bring home $400 worth of foreign goods duty free. So can each member of your family, regardless of age; and your exemptions may be pooled, so one of you can bring in more if another brings in less. A flat 10% duty applies to the next $1,000 of goods; above $1,400, the rate varies with the merchandise. (If the 48-hour or 30-day limits apply, your duty-free allowance drops to $25, which may not be pooled.) Please note that these are the *general* rules, applicable to most countries, including France.

Travelers 21 or older may bring back 1 liter of alcohol duty-free, provided the beverage laws of the state through which they reenter the United States allow it. In addition, 100 non-Cuban cigars and 200 cigarettes are allowed, regardless of your age. Antiques and works of art more than 100 years old are duty-free.

Gifts valued at less than $50 may be mailed duty free to stateside friends and relatives, with a limit of one package per day per addressee (do not send alcohol or tobacco products, nor perfume valued at more than $5). These gifts do not count as part of your exemption, unless you bring them home with you. Mark the package "Unsolicited Gift" and include the nature of the gift and its retail value.

For a copy of "Know Before You Go," a free brochure detailing what you may and may not bring back to the United States, rates of duty, and other pointers, contact the **U.S. Customs Service** (Box 7407, Washington, DC 20044, tel. 202/927–6724).

Canadian Customs

Once per calendar year, when you've been out of Canada for at least seven days, you may bring in $300 worth of goods duty-free. If you've been away less than seven days but more than 48 hours, the duty-free exemption drops to $100 but can be claimed any number of times (as can a $20 duty-free exemption for absences of 24 hours or more). You cannot combine the yearly and 48-hour exemptions, use the $300 exemption only partially (to save the balance for a later trip), or pool exemptions with family members. Goods claimed under the $300 exemption may follow you by mail; those claimed under the lesser exemptions must accompany you on your return.

Alcohol and tobacco products may be included in the yearly and 48-hour exemptions but not in the 24-hour exemption. If you meet the age requirements of the province through which you reenter Canada, you may bring in, duty free, 1.14 liters (40 imperial ounces) of wine or liquor *or* two dozen 12-ounce cans or bottles of beer or ale. If you are 16 or older, you may bring in, duty free, 200 cigarettes, 50 cigars or cigarillos, and 400 tobacco sticks or 400 grams of manufactured tobacco. Alcohol and tobacco must accompany you on your return.

Gifts may be mailed to Canada duty-free. These do not count as part of your exemption. Each gift may be worth up to $60—label the package "Unsolicited Gift—Value under $60." There are no limits on the number of gifts that may be sent per day or per addressee, but you can't mail alcohol or tobacco.

For more information, including details of duties on items that exceed your duty-free limit, ask the Revenue Canada Customs and Excise Department (Connaught Bldg., MacKenzie Ave., Ottawa, Ont., K1A OL5, tel. 613/957-0275) for a copy of the free brochure "I Declare/ Je Déclare."

U.K. Customs If your journey was wholly within EC countries, you no longer need to pass through customs when you return to the United Kingdom. According to EC guidelines, you may bring in 800 cigarettes, 400 cigarillos, 200 cigars, and 1 kilogram of smoking tobacco, plus 10 liters of spirits, 20 liters of fortified wine, 90 liters of wine, and 110 liters of beer. If you exceed these limits, you may be required to prove that the goods are for your personal use or are gifts.

For further information or a copy of "A Guide for Travellers," which details standard customs procedures as well as what you may bring into the United Kingdom from abroad, contact HM Customs and Excise (New King's Beam House, 22 Upper Ground, London SE1 9PJ, tel. 071/620–1313).

Arriving and Departing

From North America by Plane

Flights are either nonstop, direct, or connecting. A **nonstop** flight requires no change of plane and makes no stops. A **direct** flight stops at least once and can involve a change of plane, although the flight number remains the same; if the first leg is late, the second waits. This is not the case with a **connecting** flight, which involves a different plane and a different flight number.

Airlines The airlines that serve Paris from various major U.S. cities include **Air France** (tel. 800/237–2747, tel. 45–35–61–61 in Paris), **TWA** (tel. 800/892–4141, tel. 47–20–62–11 in Paris), **American Airlines** (tel. 800/433–7300, tel. 42–89–05–22 in Paris), **Delta** (tel. 800/241–4141, tel. 47–68–92–92 in Paris), **United** (tel. 800/538–2929, tel. 48–97–82–82 in Paris), **Continental** (tel. 800/231–0856, tel. 42–99–09–09 in Paris), **Northwest** (tel. 800/225–2525, tel. 42–66–90–00 in Paris) and **USAir** (tel. 800/428–4322, tel. 49–10–29–00 in Paris). Most local reservations offices are closed on Sundays.

Flying Time From New York: 7 hours. From Chicago: 9½ hours. From Los Angeles: 11 hours.

Between the Airports and Downtown *Charles de Gaulle (Roissy)* The easiest way to get into Paris is on the **RER-B** line, the suburban express train. A free shuttle bus—look for the word *navette*—runs between the two terminal buildings and the train station; it takes about 10 minutes. Trains to central Paris (Les Halles, St-Michel, Luxembourg) leave every 15 minutes. The fare (including métro connection) is 33 francs, and journey time is about 30 minutes. **Buses** run every 20 minutes between Charles de Gaulle airport and the Arc de Triomphe, with a stop at the Air France air terminal at Porte Maillot. The fare is 48 francs, and journey time is about 40 minutes. The **Roissybus,** operated by the Paris Transit

Authority, has buses every 15 minutes to rue Scribe at the Opéra; cost is 30 francs. Rush-hour traffic can make this trip slow and frustrating. **Taxis** are readily available. Journey time is around 30 minutes, depending on the traffic, and the fare is around 200 francs.

Orly Airport The easiest way to get into Paris is on the **RER-C** line, the suburban express train. Again, there's a free shuttle bus from the terminal building to the train station. Trains to Paris leave every 15 minutes. The fare is 42 francs, and journey time is about 25 minutes. A shuttle-train service, **Orlyval,** runs between the Antony RER-B station and Orly airport every 7 minutes. The fare from downtown Paris is 42 francs during peak periods, or 32 francs daily 11 AM–3 PM and after 9 PM, and Sat. noon–Sun. noon. **Buses** run every 12 minutes between Orly airport and the Air France air terminal at Les Invalides on the Left Bank. The fare is 32 francs, and journey time is between 30 and 60 minutes, depending on traffic. The Paris Transit Authority's **Orlybus** leaves every 15 minutes for the Denfert-Rochereau métro station; cost is 23 francs. **Taxis** take around 25 minutes in light traffic; the fare will be about 160 francs.

From the United Kingdom

By Plane **Air France** (tel. 081/742–6600) and **British Airways** (tel. 081/897–4000) together offer service from London's Heathrow Airport to Paris every hour to two hours. The cost of round-trip tickets is almost halved if you purchase them 14 days in advance and stay over on a Saturday night. There are three **British Airways** and up to five **Air France** flights daily, except weekends, to Paris from London's most central airport, London City, in the Docklands area.

Other airlines with regular scheduled flights from London to Paris include **British Midland** (tel. 081/754-7321), **TAT European** (tel. 0293-567955), and **Dan Air** (tel. 081/759–1818). Except on Sundays, there are several daily flights (mostly Air France and BA) direct to Paris from Manchester, Bristol, and Birmingham, and up to four from Glasgow, Edinburgh, Aberdeen, Cardiff, Belfast, Newcastle, and Southampton.

The Paris Travel Service (115 Buckingham Palace Rd., London SW1 V9SJ, tel. 071/2337892) operates a good-value weekly Paris Express from Gatwick to Beauvais (a 40-minute flight and a one-hour bus ride into central Paris). Departure is on Friday, and return is the following Monday.

By Car There are a number of different driving routes to Paris. The Dover–Calais route includes the shortest Channel crossing; the Newhaven–Dieppe route requires a longer Channel crossing but a shorter drive through France.

Dover–Calais Ticket prices for ferries vary widely depending on the number of passengers in a group, the size of the car, the season and time of day, and the length of your trip. Call one of the ferry service reservation offices for more exact information. **P&O European Ferries** (Channel House, Channel View Rd., Dover, Kent CT17 9TJ, tel. 081/575–8555) has up to 15 sailings a day; the crossing takes about 75 minutes. **Sealink** (Charter House, Park St., Ashford, Kent TN24 8EX, tel. 0233/646801) operates up to 18 sailings a day; the crossing takes about 90 minutes. **Hoverspeed** (Maybrook House, Queens Gardens, Dover, Kent CT17 9UQ, tel. 0304/240241) operates up to 23 crossings a day, and the crossing (by Hovercraft) takes 35 minutes.

Dover–Boulogne **P&O European Ferries** has up to six sailings a day with a crossing time of 100 minutes. Fares are the same as for the Dover–Calais crossing. **Hoverspeed** also operates on this route, with six 40-minute crossings a day. The fares are the same as for the Dover–Calais route.

Ramsgate–Dunkerque **Sally Line** (Argyle Centre, York St., Ramsgate, Kent CT11 9DS, tel. 0843/595522) has up to five 2½-hour crossings a day.

Newhaven–Dieppe **Sealink** has up to four sailings a day; the crossing takes four hours.

Portsmouth–Le Havre **P&O European Ferries** has up to three sailings a day, and the crossing takes 5¾ hours by day, 7 by night.

Driving distances from the French ports to Paris are as follows: **from Calais,** 290 kilometers (180 miles); **from Boulogne,** 243 kilometers (151 miles); **from Dieppe,** 193 kilometers (120 miles); **from Dunkerque,** 257 kilometers (160 miles). The fastest routes to Paris from each port are via the N43, A26, and A1 from Calais; via the N1 from Boulogne; via the N15 from Le Havre; via the D915 and N1 from Dieppe; and via the A25 and A1 from Dunkerque.

By Train **British Rail** has four departures a day from London's Victoria Station, all linking with the Dover–Calais/Boulogne ferry services through to Paris. There is also an overnight service using the Newhaven–Dieppe ferry. Journey time is about eight hours. Round-trip fare is around £65 (five-day excursion). Credit card bookings are accepted by phone (tel. 071/834–2345) or in person at a British Rail Travel Centre.

The Channel Tunnel, destined for trains only (with cars taken on board), which will slash the Paris–London journey time to under four hours, pushed back its scheduled opening date to spring 1994. Fare details were not available at press time.

Train Stations Paris has six international rail stations: **Gare du Nord** (northern France, northern Europe, and England via Calais or Boulogne); **Gare St-Lazare** (Normandy, England via Dieppe); **Gare de l'Est** (Strasbourg, Luxembourg, Basle, and central Europe); **Gare de Lyon** (Lyon, Marseille, the Riviera, Geneva, Italy); and **Gare d'Austerlitz** (Loire Valley, southwest France, Spain). Note that **Gare Montparnasse** has taken over as the main terminus for trains bound for southwest France since the introduction of the new TGV-Atlantique service. For train information from any station, call 45–82–50–50. You can reserve tickets in any Paris station, irrespective of destination. Go to the **Grandes Lignes** counter for travel within France and to the **Billets Internationaux** desk if you're heading out of France.

By Bus **Eurolines** (52 Grosvenor Gardens, London SW1W 0AU, tel. 071/730–0202) operates a daily service from London's Victoria Coach Station, via the Dover–Calais ferry, to Paris. Departures are at 9 AM, arriving at 6:15 PM; 12 noon, arriving at 9:45 PM; and 9 PM, arriving at 7:15 AM. Fares are £52 round-trip (under-25 youth pass £49), £31 one-way.

Hoverspeed (Maybrook House, Queen's Gardens, Dover, Kent CT17 9UQ, tel. 0304/240241) offers a faster journey time with up to five daily departures from Victoria Coach Station. The fare is £25 one-way, £43 round-trip.

Both the Eurolines and Hoverspeed services are bookable in person at any **National Express** office or at the **Coach Travel Centre,** 13 Regent Street, London SW1 4LR. Credit card reservations can be made by calling 071/824–8657.

Staying in Paris

Important Addresses and Numbers

Tourist Information
The main **Paris Tourist Office** (127 av. des Champs-Elysées, 75008 Paris, tel. 47–23–61–72) is open daily 9–8. There are also offices at all main train stations, except Gare St-Lazare. Dial 47–20–88–98 for recorded information in English. All of these offices—and certain métro stations—sell museum passes (*Carte Musées et Monuments*), which offer unlimited access to more than 60 museums and monuments in Paris over a one-, three-, or five-day period; cost, respectively, is 55, 110, or 160 francs.

Embassies
U.S. Embassy (2 av. Gabriel, 8e, tel. 42–96–12–02). **Canadian Embassy** (35 av. Montaigne, 8e, tel. 44–43–32–00). **British Embassy** (35 rue du Fbg St-Honoré, 8e, tel. 42–66–91–42).

Emergencies
Police (tel. 17). **Ambulance** (tel. 15 or 45–67–50–50). **Doctor** (tel. 47–07–77–77). **Dentist** (tel. 43–37–51–00).

Hospitals
The American Hospital (63 blvd. Victor Hugo, Neuilly, tel. 46–41–25–25) has a 24-hour emergency service. **The Hertford British Hospital** (3 rue Barbès, Levallois-Perret, tel. 47–58–13–12) also offers a 24-hour service.

Pharmacies
Dhéry (Galerie des Champs, 84 av. des Champs-Elysées, 8e, tel. 45–62–02–41) is open 24 hours. **Drugstore Publicis** (corner of blvd. St-Germain and rue de Rennes, 6e) is open daily till 2 AM. **Pharmacie des Arts** (106 blvd. Montparnasse, 14e) is open daily till midnight.

Tour **American Express** (11 rue Scribe, 9e, tel. 47–77–
Operators 70–00). **Air France** (119 av. des Champs-
Elysées, 8e, tel. 42–99–23–64). **Wagons-Lits** (8
rue Auber, 9e, tel. 42–66–90–90).

Telephones

To call Paris from the United States, dial 011–
33–1 and then the local eight-digit number.

Local Calls The French telephone system is modern and efficient. A local call costs 73 centimes plus 12 centimes per minute. Call-boxes are plentiful;
they're found at post offices and often in cafés.

Most French pay phones are now operated by
cards *(télécartes)*, which you can buy from post
offices and some *tabacs* (cost is 40 francs for 50
units; 96 francs for 120). These cards will save
you money and hassle. In cafés you can still find
pay phones that operate with 50-centime, 1-, 2-,
and 5-franc coins (1 franc minimum). Lift the re-
ceiver, place your coin(s) in the appropriate
slots, and dial. Unused coins are returned when
you hang up. All French phone numbers have
eight digits; a code is required only when calling
Paris from outside the city (add 16–1 for Paris)
and when calling outside the city from Paris
(add 16, then the number). Note that the number system was changed in 1985, so you may
come across some seven-figure numbers in Paris
and some six-figure ones elsewhere. Add 4 to
the start of such Paris numbers, and add the former two-figure area code to the provincial numbers.

International Dial 19 and wait for the tone, then dial the coun-
Calls try code (1 for the United States and Canada, 44
for the United Kingdom) and the area code (mi-
nus any initial 0) and number. Expect to be over-
charged if you make calls from your hotel.
Approximate daytime rates, per minute, are
9.36 francs to the United States and Canada;
4.50 francs to the United Kingdom; reduced
rates, per minute, are 5.71 francs (2 AM–noon) to
the United States and Canada or 7.17 francs (8
PM–2 AM weekdays, noon–2 AM Sun. and public
holidays); and 3 francs to the United Kingdom
(before 8 AM and after 2 PM).

AT&T's USA Direct program allows callers to take advantage of AT&T rates by connecting directly with the AT&T system. To do so from France dial 19-0011. You can then either dial direct (area code + number), billing the call to a credit card, or make a collect call.

Operators and Information To find a number within France or to request information, dial 12. For international inquiries, dial 19–33 plus the country code.

Mail

Post offices, or PTT, are scattered throughout every arrondissement, and are recognizable by a yellow sign. They are usually open weekdays 8 AM–noon and 2:30–7 PM, Sat. 8 AM–noon. The main office, 52 rue du Louvre, 1er, is open 24 hours.

Rates Airmail letters to the United States and Canada cost 4.00 francs for 20 grams, 7.30 francs for 30 grams, 7.60 francs for 40 grams, and 7.90 francs for 50 grams. Letters to the United Kingdom cost 2.50 francs for up to 20 grams, as they do within France. Postcards cost 2.30 francs within France and to Canada, the United States, the United Kingdom, and EC countries; 3.70 francs if sent to North America by airmail. Stamps can be bought in post offices and cafés sporting a red TABAC sign.

Receiving Mail If you're uncertain where you'll be staying, have mail sent to **American Express** (if you're a card member), or to **Poste Restante** at any post office.

Getting Around Paris

Paris is relatively small as capital cities go, and most of its prize monuments and museums are within easy walking distance of one another. Walking also lets you participate in the French national sport of people-watching, and gives you an appetite (and an excuse) for that next memorable meal. The most convenient form of public transportation is the métro, with stops every few hundred yards. Buses are a slower alternative, though you do see more of the city. Taxis are relatively inexpensive and convenient, but not always easy to hail. Private car travel within Paris is best avoided; parking is extremely difficult.

Maps of the métro/RER network are available free from any métro station and in many hotels. They are also posted on every platform, as are maps of the bus network. Bus routes are also marked at bus stops and on buses. To help you find your way around Paris, we suggest you buy a *Plan de Paris par arrondissement* (about 20 frs), a city guide with separate maps of each district, including the whereabouts of métro stations and an index of street names. They're on sale in newsstands, bookstores, stationers, and drugstores.

By Métro Métro stations are recognizable either by a large yellow M within a circle or by the distinctive curly green Art Nouveau railings and archway bearing the full title (Métropolitain). The métro is the most efficient way to get around Paris and is so clearly marked at all points that it's easy to find your way around without having to ask directions.

There are 13 métro lines crisscrossing Paris and the suburbs, and you are seldom more than 500 yards from the nearest station. It is essential to know the name of the last station on the line you take, as this name appears on all signs. A connection (you can make as many as you like on one ticket) is called a *correspondance*. At junction stations, illuminated orange signs bearing the name of the line terminus appear over the correct corridors for each *correspondance*. Illuminated blue signs marked *sortie* indicate the station exit.

The métro service starts at 5:30 AM and continues until 1:15 AM, when the last train on each line reaches its terminus. Some lines and stations in the less salubrious parts of Paris are a bit risky at night; in particular Lines 2 and 13. But in general, the métro is relatively safe throughout, providing you don't walk around with your wallet hanging out of your back pocket or (especially women) travel alone late at night. The biggest nuisances you're likely to come across will be the wine-swigging *clochards* (tramps) blurting out drunken songs as they bed down on platform benches.

Paris Arrondissements

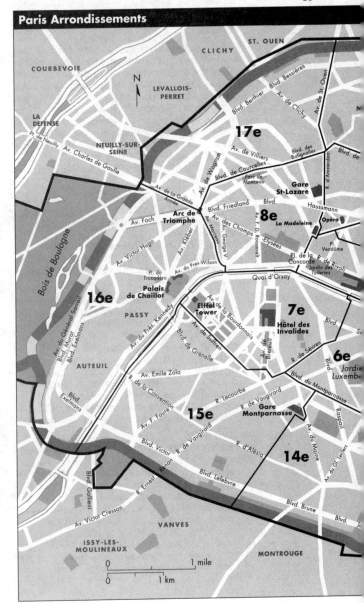

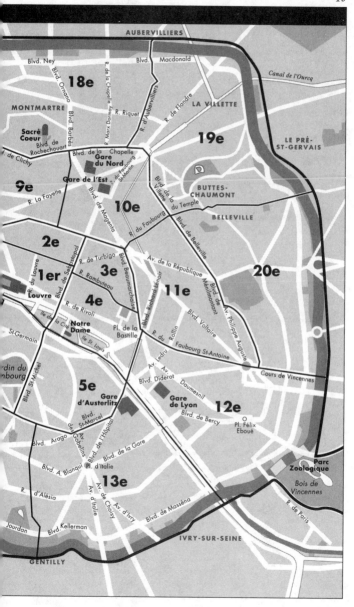

AUBERVILLIERS

Blvd. Ney
Blvd. Macdonald
Canal de l'Ourcq

18e
Blvd. Ornano

MONTMARTRE
Blvd. Barbès
R. Marx Dormoy
R. Riquet
R. d'Aubervilliers
R. de Flandre

LA VILLETTE

Sacré
Coeur
Blvd. de Rochechouart

19e

LE PRÉ-
ST-GERVAIS

Blvd. de la Chapelle
Gare
du Nord

9e
Gare de l'Est

R. La Fayette

R. du Faubourg St-Martin

10e

Blvd. de Magenta

BUTTES-
CHAUMONT
du Temple

Blvd. de la Villette

BELLEVILLE

R. du Faubourg

Blvd. de Belleville

2e

R. de Turbigo

Blvd. de Sébastopol

Av. de la République

R. du Louvre

3e
R. Rambuteau
Blvd. Beaumarchais

1er
Louvre

11e

20e

Blvd. de Ménilmontant

Av. Philippe Auguste

4e
R. de Rivoli

Blvd. Richard Lenoir

Île de la Cité
Notre
Dame

Blvd. Voltaire

St-Germain

Île St. Louis

Pl. de la
Bastille

R. du Rollin

rdin du
mbourg

Faubourg St-Antoine

Blvd. St-Michel

Av. Ledru
Av.
Daumesnil

Cours de Vincennes

5e
Gare
d'Austerlitz

Blvd. Diderot

Gare
de Lyon

12e

Blvd. de Bercy

Pl. Félix
Eboué

Blvd.
St-Marcel
Av. des Gobelins
Blvd. de l'Hôpital

**Parc
Zoologique**

Blvd. Arago

Blvd. de la Gare

Bois de
Vincennes

Blvd. A. Blanqui
Pl. d'Italie

R. de Paris

R. d'Alésia

13e

Av. de Choisy
Av. d'Italie
Av. d'Ivry
Blvd. de Masséna

Jourdan
Blvd. Kellerman

IVRY-SUR-SEINE

GENTILLY

Paris Métro

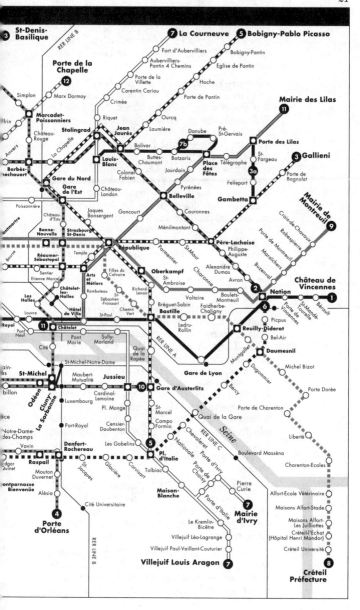

The métro network connects at several points in Paris with the **RER** network. RER trains, which race across Paris from suburb to suburb, are a sort of supersonic métro and can be great time-savers.

All métro tickets and passes are valid for RER *and* bus travel within Paris. Métro tickets cost 6.50 francs each, though a carnet (10 tickets for 39 francs) is better value. If you're staying for a week or more and plan to use the métro frequently, the best deal is the weekly *(coupon jaune)* or monthly *(carte orange)* ticket, sold according to zone. Zones 1 and 2 cover the entire métro network; tickets cost 59 francs a week or 208 francs a month. If you plan to take suburban trains to visit places in the Ile-de-France, we suggest you consider a four-zone (Versailles, St-Germain-en-Laye; 109 francs a week) or six-zone (Rambouillet, Fontainebleau; 142 francs a week) ticket. For these weekly/monthly tickets, you will need a pass (available from rail and major métro stations) and two passport-size photographs.

Alternatively, there are one-day *(Formule 1)* and two-, three-, and five-day *(Paris Visite)* unlimited travel tickets for the métro, bus, and RER. Their advantage is that, unlike the *coupon jaune*, which is good from Monday morning to Sunday evening, *Formule 1* and *Paris Visite* passes are valid starting any day of the week and also give you discounts on a limited number of museums and tourist attractions. The price is 36 (one-day), 65 (two-day), 90 (three-day), and 145 (five-day) francs for Paris only; 85, 150, 200, and 275 francs, respectively, for suburbs including Versailles, St-Germain-en-Laye, and Euro Disney.

Access to métro and RER platforms is through an automatic ticket barrier. Slide your ticket in and pick it up as it pops out. Keep your ticket during your journey; you'll need it to leave the RER system.

By Bus Travel by bus is a convenient, though slower, way to get around the city. Paris buses are green single-deckers; route number and destination are marked in front and with major stopping-places along the sides. Most routes operate from 6 AM to 8:30 PM; some continue to midnight. Ten night buses operate hourly (1:30–5:30 AM) between Châtelet and various nearby suburbs; they can be stopped by hailing them at any point on their route. The brown bus shelters, topped by red and yellow circular signs, contain timetables and route maps.

The bus accepts métro tickets, or you can buy a single ticket on board. You need to show (but not punch) weekly, monthly, and *Paris-Visite/Formule 1* tickets to the driver as you get on. If you have individual yellow tickets, you should state your destination and be prepared to punch one or more tickets in the red and gray machines on board the bus.

By Taxi Paris taxis may not have the charm of their London counterparts—there is no standard vehicle or color—but they're cheaper. Daytime rates (7 AM till 7 PM) within Paris are around 2.80 francs per kilometer, and nighttime rates are around 4.50 francs. There is a basic hire charge of 11 francs for all rides, and a 5-franc supplement per piece of luggage. Rates outside the city limits are about 40% higher. Waiting time is charged at roughly 100 francs per hour. You are best off asking your hotel or restaurant to ring for a taxi, or going to the nearest taxi station (you can find one every couple of blocks); cabs with their signs lit can be hailed, but are annoyingly difficult to spot. Note that taxis seldom take more than three people at a time. Tip the driver about 10%.

By Bike You can hire bikes in the Bois de Boulogne (Jardin d'Acclimatation), Bois de Vincennes, some RER stations, and from the Bateaux-Mouches embarkation point by place de l'Alma. Or try **Paris-Vélo** (2 rue du Fer à Moulin, 5e, tel. 43–37–59–22). Rental rates vary from about 90 to 140 francs per day, 160 to 220 francs per weekend, and 420 to 500 francs per week, depending on the type of bike. There is about a 1,000-franc deposit for rental.

Guided Tours

Orientation Tours Bus tours of Paris offer a good introduction to the city. The two largest operators are **City-**

rama (4 pl. des Pyramides, 1er, tel. 42–60–30–
14) and **Paris Vision** (214 rue de Rivoli, 1er, tel.
42–60–31–25). Their tours start from the place
des Pyramides, across from the Louvre end of
the Tuileries Gardens. Tours are generally in
double-decker buses with either a live or tape-
recorded commentary (English, of course, is
available) and last three hours. Expect to pay
about 150 francs.

The **RATP** (Paris Transport Authority, tel. 40–
46–42–17) has many guide-accompanied excur-
sions in and around Paris. Inquire at its Tourist
Service on the place de la Madeleine, 8e (to the
right of the church as you face it) or at the office
at 53 bis quai des Grands-Augustins, 6e. Both
are open daily 9–5.

Special-Interest **Cityrama** and **Paris Vision** (*see* Orientation
Tours Tours, *above*) offer a variety of thematic tours
("Historic Paris," "Modern Paris," "Paris-by-
Night") lasting from 2½ hours to all day and
costing between 150 and 300 francs (more if ad-
mission to a cabaret show is included).

Bike Tours **Paris by Cycle** (99 rue de la Jonquière, 17e, tel.
42–63–36–63) organizes daily bike tours around
Paris and its environs (Versailles, Chantilly,
and Fontainebleau) for about 180 francs (an additional 95 francs for bike rental).

Boat Trips Boat trips along the Seine, usually lasting about
an hour, are a must for the first-time visitor.
Many boats have powerful floodlights to illuminate riverbank buildings; on some, you can also
lunch or wine and dine—book ahead. The following services operate regularly throughout
the day and in the evening.

Bateaux-Mouches has departures from Pont de
l'Alma (Right Bank), 8e, tel. 42–25–96–10.
Boats depart 10–noon, 2–7, and 8:30–10:30. The
price is 30 francs (40 francs after 8 PM; 15 francs
children under 14). Lunch is served on the 1 PM
boat and costs 300 francs (150 francs children
under 14). Dinner on the 8:30 service costs 500
francs (reservations required; no children).
Wine and service are included in the lunch and
dinner prices.

Vedettes du Pont Neuf has departures from
Square du Vert Galant (Ile de la Cité), 1er, tel.

46–33–98–38. Boats depart 10–noon, 1:30–6:30, and 9–10:30 every half hour. The price is 40 francs during the day (20 francs children under 10 and 40 francs at night).

Bateaux Parisiens–Tour Eiffel has departures from Pont d'Iéna (Left Bank), 7e, tel. 44–11–33–44. Boats depart at 10 and 11 AM and 12, 2, 3, 4, 5, and 6 PM. The price is 40 francs during the day (20 francs children under 12). Lunch service costs 300 francs (200 francs children under 12). Dinner cruises on the 8 PM service cost 550 francs (no children). Wine and service are included in the lunch and dinner prices.

Canauxrama (tel. 42–39–15–00) organizes leisurely half-day canal tours in flat-bottom barges along the picturesque but relatively unknown St-Martin and Ourcq Canals in East Paris. Departures are from 5 bis quai de la Loire, 19e (9:15 and 2:45), or from Bassin de l'Arsenal, 12e (9:45 and 2:30), opposite 50 boulevard de la Bastille. The price is 70 francs (60 francs for students and senior citizens and on weekend afternoons; 45 francs children under 12).

Food Tours   If you have more than a passing interest in French cuisine, you may be interested in **Paris en Cuisine** (49 rue de Richelieu, 1er, tel. 42–61–35–23). American Robert Noah leads individuals and groups on walking tours of the Rungis wholesale food market, as well as various restaurant and tasting outings.

Walking Tours   There are plenty of guided tours of specific areas of Paris, often concentrating on a historical or architectural topic—"Restored Mansions of the Marais," "Private Walled Gardens in St-Germain," or "Secret Parts of the Invalides." Tours are often restricted to 30 people and are popular with Parisians as well as tourists. They are accompanied by guides whose enthusiasm and dedication is invariably exemplary, though most are French and may not be able to communicate their enthusiasm to you in English. These potential linguistic problems are more than outweighed by the chance to see Paris in a new light and to visit buildings and monuments that are not usually open to the public. Charges vary between 35 and 50 francs, depending on fees that may be needed to visit certain buildings. Tours last around two hours and are generally held in the afternoons, starting at 2:30 or 3. Details are published in the weekly magazines *Pariscope* and *L'Officiel des Spectacles* under the heading "Conférences." In most cases, you must simply turn up at the meeting point (usually listed as "RV" or "rendezvous"), but it's best to get there early in case of restriction on numbers. You can get information on walking tours by contacting the **Caisse Nationale des Monuments Historiques** (Bureau des Visites/Conférences, Hôtel de Sully, 62 rue St-Antoine, 4e, tel. 44–61–20–00), which publishes a small booklet every two months listing all upcoming tours. For visits to some private mansions, you may be asked to show identification, so be sure to have your passport with you.

Personal Guides **Espaces Limousine** (18 rue Vignon, 9e, tel. 42–65–63–16) and **Executive Car** (25 rue d'Astorg, 8e, tel. 42–65–54–20) have limousines and minibuses (taking up to seven passengers) that will take you around Paris and environs for a minimum of three hours. Reservations are required. The cost is about 250 francs per hour.

Opening and Closing Times

Banks are open weekdays, but there's no strict pattern to their hours of business. Generally, they're open from 9:30 to 4:30 or 5. Some banks close for lunch between 12:30 and 2.

Most Paris **museums** close one day a week—usually either Monday or Tuesday—and on national holidays. Usually, they're open from 10 to 5 or 6. Many museums close for lunch (12 to 2) and are open Sundays only in the afternoon.

Large **shops** are open from 9 or 9:30 to 6 or 7 and don't close at lunchtime. Smaller shops often open earlier (8 AM) but take a lengthy lunch break (1 to 4); small food shops are often open Sunday mornings, 9 to 1. Some corner grocery stores will stay open until about 10 PM. Most shops close all day Monday.

2 Exploring Paris

Paris is a city of vast, noble perspectives and winding, hidden streets. This combination of the pompous and the intimate is a particularly striking and alluring feature of Paris. The French capital is also, for the tourist, a practical city: It is relatively small as capitals go, with many of its major sites and museums within walking distance of one another.

In fact, the best method of getting to know Paris is on foot, although public transportation—particularly the métro subway system—is excellent. Buy a *Plan de Paris* booklet: a city map-guide with a street-name index that also shows métro stations. Note that all métro stations have a detailed neighborhood map just inside the entrance.

Paris owes both its development and much of its visual appeal to the river Seine, which weaves through its heart. Each bank of the Seine has its own personality; the Rive Droite (Right Bank), with its spacious boulevards and haughty buildings, generally has a more sober and genteel feeling to it than the more carefree and bohemian Rive Gauche (Left Bank) to the south.

Paris's historical and geographical heart is Notre Dame Cathedral on the Ile de la Cité, the larger of the Seine's two islands (the other is the Ile St-Louis). The city's principal tourist axis is less than 4 miles long, running parallel to the north bank of the Seine from the Arc de Triomphe to the Bastille.

Monuments and museums are sometimes closed for lunch, usually between 12 and 2, and one day a week, usually Monday or Tuesday. Check before you set off. And don't forget that cafés in Paris are open all day long. They are a great boon to foot-weary tourists in need of a coffee, a beer, or a sandwich. *Boulangeries* (bakeries) are another reliable source of sustenance.

The Historic Heart

Numbers in the margin correspond to points of interest on the Historic Heart map.

Of the two islands in the Seine—the Ile St-Louis (*see* The Marais and Ile St-Louis, *below*) and Ile de la Cité—it is the Ile de la Cité that forms the historic heart of Paris. It was here, for obvious reasons of defense, and in the hope of controlling the trade that passed along the Seine, that the earliest inhabitants of Paris, the Gaulish tribe of the Parisii, settled in about 250 BC. They called their little home Lutetia, meaning "settlement surrounded by water." Whereas the Ile St-Louis is today largely residential, the Ile de la Cité remains deeply historic, the result not just of more than 2,000 years of habitation, but of the fact that this is the site of the most important and one of the most beautiful churches in France—the great brooding cathedral of Notre Dame. Few of the island's other medieval buildings have survived to the present, most having fallen victim to town planner Baron Haussmann's ambitious rebuilding of the city in the mid-19th century. But among the rare survivors are the jewel-like Sainte-Chapelle, a vision of shimmering stained glass, and the Conciergerie, the grim former city prison.

Another major attraction on this tour—the Louvre—came into existence in the mid-13th century, when Philippe-Auguste built it as a fortress to protect the city's western flank. It was not until pleasure-loving François I began a partial rebuilding of this original rude fortress in the early 16th century that today's Louvre began gradually to take shape. A succession of French rulers was responsible for this immense, symmetrical structure, now the largest museum in the world, as well as the easiest to get lost in.

Toward the Louvre

The tour begins at the western tip of the Ile de la Cité, at the sedate **Square du Vert Galant**. Nothing is controversial here, not even the statue of the Vert Galant himself, literally the vigorous—by which was really meant the amorous—adventurer, Henri IV, sitting foursquare on his horse. Henri, king of France from 1589 until his assassination in 1610, is probably best remembered for his cynical remark that *Paris vaut bien une messe* ("Paris is worth a mass"), a reference to his readiness to renounce his Protestantism as a condition of gaining the throne of predominantly Catholic France, and indeed of being

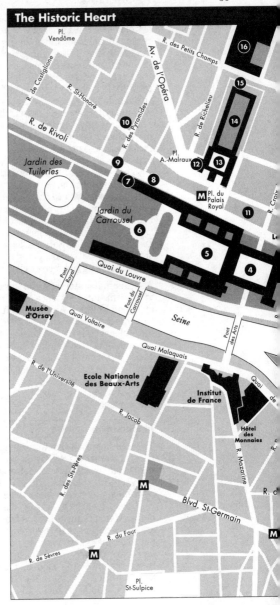

The Historic Heart

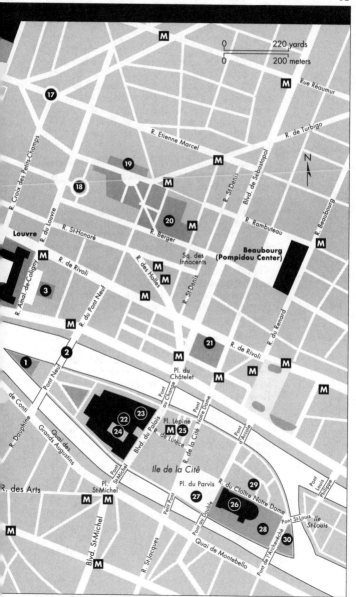

M

0 — 220 yards
0 — 200 meters

M Rue Réaumur

(17)

R. de Turbigo

R. Étienne Marcel

M

(19)

R. St-Denis

Blvd. de Sébastopol

N

(18)

(20) **M**

R. Berger

R. Rambuteau

R. Croix des Petits-Champs

R. du Louvre

R. St-Honoré

Louvre

M

R. de Rivoli

(3)

R. Amal-de-Coligny

Sq. des Innocents

R. des Halles

M M

M

St-Denis

**Beaubourg
(Pompidou Center)**

M

R. du Renard

R. Beaubourg

M

R. du Pont Neuf

M

(21) R. de Rivoli

M

(1)

(2)

Pont Neuf

M

de Conti

R. Dauphine

Quai des Grands Augustins

Pl. du Châtelet

M

Pont au Change

Pont du Palais

Pont Notre Dame

Pont d'Arcole

(22) (23)

(24)

Blvd. du Palais

Pl. Lépine

(25) **M**

R. de Lutèce

R. de la Cité

Ile de la Cité

Pont St-Michel

R. des Arts

Pl. St-Michel

M M

Blvd. St-Michel

M

R. St-Jacques

Petit Pont

Pl. du Parvis

(27)

R. du Cloître Notre Dame

(29)

(26)

(28)

Pont au Double

Quai de Montebello

Pont de l'Archevêché

Pont St-Louis

Pont Louis Phillippe

Ile St-Louis

(30)

allowed to enter the city. A measure of his canny statesmanship was provided by his enactment of the Edict of Nantes in 1598, by which French Protestants were accorded (almost) equal rights with their Catholic counterparts. It was Louis XIV's renunciation of the Edict nearly 100 years later that led to the massive Huguenot exodus from France, greatly to the economic disadvantage of the country. The square itself is a fine spot to linger on a sunny afternoon. It is also the departure point for the glass-topped *vedette* tour boats on the Seine.

Crossing the Ile de la Cité, just behind the Vert Galant, is the oldest bridge in Paris, confusingly called the **Pont Neuf**, or New Bridge. It was completed in the early 17th century and was the first bridge in the city to be built without houses lining either side. Turn left onto it. Visible to the north of the river is the large-windowed **Samaritaine** department store. Once across the river, turn left again and walk down to rue Amiral-de-Coligny. Opposite you is the massive eastern facade of the Louvre. It is Baroque dignity and coherence with no frills, a suitably imposing entrance to the rigorous classicism of the Cour Carrée beyond.

However, before heading for the Louvre, stay on the right-hand sidewalk and duck into the church of **St-Germain l'Auxerrois**. This was the French royal family's Paris church, used by them right up to 1789, in the days before the Revolution, when the Louvre was a palace rather than a museum. The fluid stonework of the facade reveals the influence of 15th-century Flamboyant Gothic, the final, exuberant fling of the Gothic before the classical takeover of the Renaissance. Notice the unusually wide windows in the nave, light flooding through them, and the equally unusual double aisles. The triumph of classicism is evident, however, in the fluted columns around the choir, the area surrounding the altar. These were added in the 18th century and are characteristic of the desire of 18th-century clerics to dress up medieval buildings in the architectural raiment of their day.

The Louvre

The best times to visit the Louvre are during lunchtime between 12:30 and 2:30 or on Monday and Wednesday evenings, when it stays open till 9:45.

In 1984, President François Mitterrand launched his Grand Louvre Project, a plan for restoration of the museum that includes the extension and modernization of the museum interior, renovation of the Palais du Louvre, and the restoration of the Carrousel gardens between the museum and the Tuileries Gardens. The project is not scheduled for completion until 1996, so don't be surprised to see construction crews and steam shovels marring the otherwise superb locale when you visit.

The Louvre colonnade across the road from St-Germain l'Auxerrois screens one of Europe's most dazzling courtyards, the **Cour Carrée,** a monumental, harmonious, and superbly rhythmical ensemble. It has something of the assured feel of an Oxford or Cambridge quadrangle, though on a much grander scale. In the **crypt** under it, excavated in 1984, sections of the defensive towers of the original, 13th-century fortress can be seen.

If you enter the museum via the quai du Louvre entrance, saunter through the courtyard and pass under the **Pavillon de l'Horloge**—the Clock Tower—and you come face to face with the Louvre's most controversial development, I. M. Pei's notorious **glass pyramid,** surrounded by three smaller pyramids. It's more than just a grandiloquent gesture, a desire on the part of Mitterrand, who commissioned it, to make his mark on the city. First, the pyramid marks the new, and much needed, entrance to the Louvre; it also houses a large museum shop, café, and restaurant. Second, it acts as the terminal point for the most celebrated city view in Europe, a majestic vista stretching through the Arc du Carrousel, the Tuileries Gardens, across place de la Concorde, up the Champs-Elysées to the towering Arc de Triomphe, and ending at the giant modern arch at La Tête Défense, 2½ miles more to the east. Needless to say, the architectural collision between classical stone blocks and pseudo-Egyptian glass panels has caused a furor. Before making up your mind, however, it may help to remember that the surrounding buildings in this part of the Louvre are mainly earnest 19th-century pastiche, whose pompous solemnity neither jars nor excites.

Paintings, drawings, antiquities, sculpture, furniture, coins, jewelry—the quality and the sheer variety are intimidating. The number-one attraction for most is Leonardo da Vinci's enigmatic *Mona Lisa*, "La Joconde" to the French. But there are numerous other works of equal quality. The collections are divided into seven sections: Oriental antiquities; Egyptian antiquities; Greek and Roman antiquities; sculpture; paintings, prints, and drawings; furniture; and objets d'art. Try to make repeat visits—the Louvre is half-price on Sundays. With the rearrangement of the museum far from complete— the rue de Rivoli wing, which used to house the French Finance Ministry, is to become part of the museum by 1994—it's not possible to say with certainty just what works will be on display where. Study the plans at the entrance to get your bearings, and pick up a map to take with you. *Tel. 40-20-50-50. Palais du Louvre. Admission: 35 frs adults, 20 frs 18-25 years, over 60, and Sun.; children under 18 free. Open Thurs.-Sun. 9-6, Mon. and Wed. 9 AM-9:45 PM. Some sections open some days only.*

Time Out If you can make it to the Tuileries, stop at **Angelina** (226 rue de Rivoli). Founded in 1903, this elegant salon de thé is famous for its "L'Africain"—a cup of hot chocolate so thick you'll need a fork to eat it (irresistible even in the summer). Non-chocoholics can select from a dizzying assortment of pastries and other goodies.

North of the Louvre

Stretching westward from the main entrance to the Louvre and the glass pyramid is an expanse of stately, formal gardens. These are the **Tuileries Gardens** (*see* From the Arc de Triomphe to the Opéra, *below*). Leading to them is the **Arc du Carrousel,** a small relation of the distant Arc de

Triomphe and, like its big brother, put up by
Napoléon. To the north, in the Pavillon de
Marsan, the northernmost wing of the Louvre,
❼ is the **Musée des Arts Décoratifs,** which houses
over 50,000 objects charting the course of
French furniture and applied arts through the
centuries. The Musée de la Publicité, with its
collection of 50,000 posters, stages temporary
exhibits within the museum. *107 rue de Rivoli.
Admission: 23 frs. Open Wed.–Sat. 12:30–6,
Sun. 12–6.*

Running the length of the Louvre's northern
❽ side is Napoléon's elegant, arcaded **rue de
Rivoli,** a street whose generally dull tourist
shops add little to their surroundings. Cross it
❾ and you're in **place des Pyramides** and face-to-
face with its gilded statue of Joan of Arc on
horseback. The square is a focal point for city
tour buses.

Walk up rue des Pyramides and take the first
left, rue St-Honoré, to the Baroque church of
❿ **St-Roch.** The church was begun in 1653 but completed only in the 1730s, the decade of the coolly
classical facade. Classical playwright Corneille
(1606–1684) is buried here; a commemorative
plaque honoring him is located at the left of the
entrance. It's worth having a look inside the
church to see the bombastically baroque altar-
piece in the circular Lady Chapel at the far end.

Double back along rue St-Honoré to place du Palais-Royal. On the far side of the square, oppo-
⓫ site the Louvre, is the **Louvre des Antiquaires,** a
chic shopping mall housing upscale antiques
shops. It's a minimuseum in itself. Its stylish,
glass-walled corridors deserve a browse whether you intend to buy or not.

Retrace your steps to place André-Malraux,
with its exuberant fountains. The Opéra building is visible down the avenue of the same name,
while, on one corner of the square, at rue de
⓬ Richelieu, is the **Comédie Française.** This theater is the time-honored setting for performances
of classical French drama, with tragedies by Racine and Corneille and comedies by Molière regularly on the bill. The building itself dates from
1790, but the Comédie Française company was
created by that most theatrical of French mon-

archs, Louis XIV, back in 1680. Those who understand French and who have a taste for the mannered, declamatory style of French acting—it's a far cry from method acting—will appreciate an evening here. (*See* The Arts and Nightlife, Chapter 6, for details on how to get tickets.)

To the right of the theater is the unobtrusive entrance to the gardens of the **Palais-Royal.** The buildings of this former palace—royal only in that all-powerful Cardinal Richelieu (1585–1642) magnanimously bequeathed them to Louis XIII—date from the 1630s. In his early days as king, Louis XIV preferred the relative intimacy of the Palais-Royal to the intimidating splendor of the Louvre. He soon decided, though, that his own intimidating splendor warranted a more majestic setting; hence, of course, that final word in un-intimacy, Versailles.

Today, the Palais-Royal is home to the French Ministry of Culture and is not open to the public. But don't miss the **Jardin du Palais-Royal,** gardens bordered by arcades harboring discreet boutiques and divided by rows of perfectly trimmed little trees. They are a surprisingly little-known oasis in the gray heart of the city. It's hard to imagine anywhere more delightful for dozing in the afternoon sun. As you walk into the gardens, there's not much chance that you'll miss the black-and-white striped columns in the courtyard or the revolving silver spheres that slither around in the two fountains at either end, the controversial work of architect Daniel Buren. Everyone will muse on the days when this dignified spot was the haunt of prostitutes and gamblers, a veritable sink of vice, in fact. It's hard to imagine anywhere much more respectable these days. Walk up to the end, away from the main palace, and peek into the opulent, Belle Epoque, glass-lined interior of **Le Grand Véfour.** This is more than just one of the swankiest restaurants in the city; it's probably the most sumptuously appointed, too (*see* Chapter 4).

Around the corner from here, on rue de Richelieu, stands France's national library, the **Bibliothèque Nationale.** It contains over 7 million printed volumes. A copy of every book and periodical printed in France must, by law, be sent here. Visitors can admire Robert de Cotte's 18th-century courtyard and peep into the 19th-century reading room. The library galleries stage exhibits from time to time from the collections. *58 rue de Richelieu. Open daily 10–8.*

From the library, walk southeast along rue des Petits-Champs to the circular **place des Victoires.** It was laid out in 1685 by Mansart, a leading proponent of 17th-century French classicism, in honor of the military victories of Louis XIV. Louis is shown prancing on a plunging steed in the center of the square; it's a copy, put up in 1822 to replace the original one destroyed in the Revolution. You'll find some of the city's most upscale fashion shops here and on the surrounding streets.

Head south down rue Croix des Petits-Champs. You'll pass the undistinguished bulk of the Banque de France on your right. The second street on the left leads to the circular, 18th-century **Bourse du Commerce,** or Commercial Exchange. Alongside it is a 100-foot-high fluted column, all that remains of a mansion built here in 1572 for Catherine de Médicis. The column is said to have been used as a platform for stargazing by Catherine's astrologer, Ruggieri.

You don't need to scale Ruggieri's column to be able to spot the bulky outline of the church of **St-Eustache,** away to the left. Since the demolition of the 19th-century iron and glass market halls at the beginning of the '70s, an act that has since come to be seen as little short of vandalism, St-Eustache has re-emerged as a dominant element on the central Paris skyline. It is a huge church, the "cathedral" of Les Halles, built, as it were, as the market people's Right Bank reply to Notre Dame on the Ile de la Cité. St-Eustache dates from a couple of hundred years later than Notre Dame. With the exception of the feeble west front, added between 1754 and 1788, construction lasted from 1532 to 1637, spanning the twilight of Gothic and the rise of the Renaissance. As a consequence, the church is a curious architectural hybrid. Its exterior flying buttresses, for example, are solidly Gothic. Its column orders, rounded arches, and comparatively simple and thick window tracery are unmistakably classical. Few buildings bear such eloquent witness to stylistic transition. St-Eustache also features occasional organ concerts. *2 rue du Jour, tel. 46–27–89–21, for concert information. Open daily.*

The once-grimy facades of the buildings facing Les Halles have been expensively spruced up to reflect the mood of the shiny new **Forum des Halles,** the multilevel mall. Just how long the plastic, concrete, glass, and mock-marble of this gaudy mall will stay shiny is anyone's guess. Much of the complex is already showing signs of wear and tear, a state of affairs not much helped by the hordes of down-and-outs who invade it toward dusk. Nonetheless, the multitude of shops gathered at the Forum makes it somewhere no serious shopper will want to miss. The sweeping white staircase and glass reflections of the central courtyard have a certain photogenic appeal.

Leave by square des Innocents to the southeast; its 16th-century Renaissance fountain has recently been restored. As you make your way toward boulevard de Sébastopol, you can see the futuristic funnels of the Beaubourg jutting above the surrounding buildings (*see* The Marais and Ile St-Louis, *below*). Head right, toward the Seine. Just before you reach place du Châtelet on the river, you'll see the **Tour St-Jacques** to your left. This richly worked, 170-foot stump, now used for meteorological purposes and not open to the public, is all that remains of a 16th-century church destroyed in 1797.

Time Out   Just north of place du Châtelet, at 4 rue St-Denis, is **Le Trappiste.** Twenty different international beers are available on draft here, as well as more than 180 in bottles.

The Ile de la Cité

From place du Châtelet, cross back over the Seine on the Pont au Change to the Ile de la Cité. To your right looms the imposing **Palais de Justice,** the Law Courts, built by Baron Haussmann in his characteristically weighty classical style about 1860. You can wander around the building, watching the bustle of the lawyers, or attend a court hearing. But the real interest here is the medieval part of the complex, spared by Haussmann in his otherwise wholesale destruction of the lesser medieval buildings of the Ile de la Cité. There are two buildings you'll want to see: the Conciergerie and the Sainte-Chapelle.

㉓ The **Conciergerie,** the northernmost part of the complex, was originally part of the royal palace on the island. Most people know it, however, as a prison, the grim place of confinement for Danton, Robespierre, and, most famously, Marie Antoinette during the French Revolution. From here, all three, and countless others who fell foul of the Revolutionary leaders, were taken off to place de la Concorde and the guillotine. The name of the building is derived from the governor, or *concierge*, of the palace, whose considerable income was swollen by the privilege he enjoyed of renting out shops and workshops. Inside, you'll see the guardroom, complete with hefty Gothic vaulting and intricately carved columns, and the Salle des Gens d'Armes, an even more striking example of Gothic monumentality. From there, a short corridor leads to the kitchen, with its four vast fireplaces. The cells, including that in which Marie Antoinette was held, and the chapel, where objects connected with the ill-fated queen are displayed, complete the tour. *Admission: 25 frs adults, 16 frs students and senior citizens. Joint ticket with Sainte-Chapelle: 40 frs. Open daily 9:30–6:30, 10–4:30 in winter.*

㉔ The other perennial crowd puller in the Palais de Justice is the **Sainte-Chapelle,** the Holy Chapel. It was built by the genial and pious Louis IX (1226–1270), whose good works ensured his subsequent canonization. He constructed it to house what he took to be the Crown of Thorns from Christ's crucifixion and fragments of the True Cross, all of which he had bought from the impoverished Emperor Baldwin of Constantinople at phenomenal expense. Architecturally, for all its delicate and ornate exterior decoration—notice the open latticework of the pencil-like *flèche*, or spire, on the roof—the design of the building is simplicity itself. In essence, it's no more than a thin, rectangular box, much taller than it is wide. But think of it first and foremost as an oversize reliquary, an ornate medieval casket designed to house holy relics.

The building is actually two chapels in one. The plainer, first-floor chapel, made gloomy by insensitive mid-19th-century restorations (which could do with restoration themselves), was for servants and lowly members of the court. The upper chapel, infinitely more spectacular, was for the king and more important members of the court. This is what you come to see. You reach it up a dark spiral staircase. Here, again, some clumsy 19th-century work has added a deadening touch, but the glory of the chapel—the stained glass—is spectacularly intact. The chapel is airy and diaphanous, the walls glowing and sparkling as light plays on the windows. Notice how the walls, in fact, consist of at least twice as much glass as masonry: The entire aim of the architects was to provide the maximum amount of window space. The Sainte-Chapelle is one of the supreme achievements of the Middle Ages and will be a highlight of your visit to Paris. Come early in the day to avoid the dutiful crowds that trudge around it. Better still, try to attend one of the regular, candle-lit concerts given here. *Tel. 43–54–30–09, for concert information. Admission: 25 frs adults, 14 frs students and senior citizens. Joint ticket with Conciergerie: 40 frs. Open daily 9:30–6:30; winter, daily 10–5.*

② Take rue de Lutèce opposite the Palais de Justice down to place Louis-Lépine and the bustling **Marché aux Fleurs,** the flower market. There's an astoundingly wide range of flowers on sale and, on Sundays, there are birds, too—everything from sparrows to swans. *Open daily 9–7.*

Notre Dame

Around the corner, looming above the large, traffic-free place du Parvis (*kilometre zéro* to the French, the spot from which all distances to and from the city are officially measured), is the most enduring symbol of Paris, its historic and

26 geographic heart, the **Cathédrale Notre Dame.**
The building was started in 1163, with an army
of stonemasons, carpenters, and sculptors
working on a site that had previously seen a Roman temple, an early Christian basilica, and a
Romanesque church. The chancel and altar were
consecrated in 1182, but the magnificent sculptures surrounding the main doors were not put
into position until 1240. The north tower was
finished 10 years later.

Full-scale restoration started in the middle of
the century, the most conspicuous result of
which was the construction of the spire, the
flèche, over the roof. It was then, too, that
Haussmann demolished the warren of little
buildings in front of the cathedral, creating the
27 place du Parvis. The **Crypte Archéologique,** the
archaeological museum under the square, contains remains unearthed during excavations
here in the 1960s. Slides and models detail the
history of the Ile de la Cité. The foundations of
the 3rd-century Gallo-Roman rampart and of
the 6th-century Merovingian church can also be
seen. *Place du Parvis. Admission: 25 frs adults
(40 frs including tower of Notre Dame), 14 frs
age 18–24 and over 60, 6 frs age 7–17. Open daily 10–6:30, 10–5 in winter.*

Visit the place du Parvis early in the morning,
when the cathedral is at its lightest and least
crowded. You come first to the massive, 12th-
century columns supporting the twin towers.
Look down the nave to the transepts—the arms
of the church—where, at the south (right) entrance to the chancel, you'll glimpse the haunt-
ing, 12th-century statue of Notre Dame de
Paris, Our Lady of Paris. The chancel itself owes
parts of its decoration to a vow taken by Louis
XIII in 1638. Still without an heir after 23 years
of marriage, he promised to dedicate the entire
country to the Virgin Mary if his queen produced a son. When the longed-for event came to
pass, Louis set about redecorating the chancel
and choir.

On the south side of the chancel is the **Treasury,**
with a collection of garments, reliquaries, and
silver and gold plate. *Admission: 15 frs adults,*

10 frs students and senior citizens, 5 frs children. Open daily 10–5:45.

The 387-step climb to the top of the **towers** is worth the effort for the close-up view of the famous gargoyles—most of them added in the 19th century—and the expansive view over the city. *Entrance via north tower. Admission: 30 frs adults, 16 frs students and senior citizens. Open daily 10–4:30.*

On the subject of views, no visit to Notre Dame is complete without a walk behind the cathedral to **Square Jean XXIII**, located between the river and the building. It offers a breathtaking sight of the east end of the cathedral, ringed by flying buttresses, surmounted by the spire. From here, the building seems almost to float above the Seine like some vast, stone ship.

If your interest in the cathedral is not yet sated, duck into the **Musée Notre Dame.** It displays paintings, engravings, medallions, and other objects and documents, all of which trace the cathedral's history. *10 rue du Cloître-Notre-Dame. Admission: 10 frs, 6 frs students and senior citizens, 4 frs children under 14. Open Wed. and weekends only, 2:30–6.*

There's a final pilgrimage you may like to make on the Ile de la Cité to the **Mémorial de la Déportation,** located at square de l'Ile-de-France, at the eastern tip of the island. Here, in what was once the city morgue, you'll find the modern crypt, dedicated to those French men and women who died in Nazi concentration camps. You may find a visit to the quiet garden above it a good place to rest and to muse on the mysterious dichotomy that enables the human race to construct buildings of infinite beauty and to treat its fellow men with infinite cruelty. *Admission free. Open daily 9–6, 9–dusk in winter.*

The Marais and Ile St-Louis

Numbers in the margin correspond to points of interest on the Marais and Ile St-Louis map.

This tour includes two of the oldest and most historic neighborhoods in Paris: the Marais—once a marshy area north of the Seine, today about the most sought-after residential and business district of the city—and the Ile St-Louis, the smaller of the two islands in the Seine. It also includes a side trip to the Bastille, site of the infamous prison stormed on July 14, 1789, an event that came to symbolize the beginning of the French Revolution. Largely in commemoration of the bicentennial of the Revolution in 1989, the Bastille area has been renovated.

Renovation is one of the key notes of this tour, especially around the Marais; the word *marais*, incidentally, means marsh or swamp. Well into the '70s, this was one of the city's poorest areas, filled with dilapidated tenement buildings and squalid courtyards. Today, most of the Marais's spectacular *hôtels particuliers*—loosely, "mansions," one-time residences of aristocratic families—have been restored and transformed into museums. The grubby streets of the Jewish quarter, around the rue des Rosiers, is about the only area to remain undeveloped. The area's regeneration was sparked by the building of the Beaubourg, arguably Europe's most vibrant—and architecturally whimsical—cultural center. The gracious architecture of the 17th and early 18th centuries, however, sets the tone for the rest of the Marais. Try to visit during the Festival du Marais, held every June and July, when concerts, theater, and ballet are performed.

Hôtel de Ville to Beaubourg

❶ Begin your tour at the **Hôtel de Ville,** the city hall, overlooking the Seine. In the Commune of 1871, the Hôtel de Ville was burned to the ground. Today's exuberant building, based closely on the Renaissance original, went up between 1874 and 1884. In 1944, following the lib-

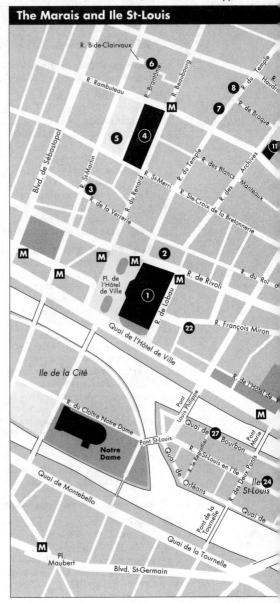

The Marais and Ile St-Louis

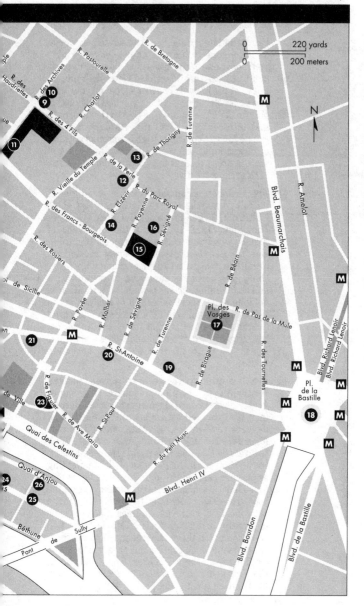

eration of Paris from Nazi rule, General de Gaulle took over the leadership of France here.

From the Hôtel de Ville, head north across rue de Rivoli and up rue du Temple. On your right, you'll pass one of the city's most popular department stores, the **Bazar de l'Hôtel de Ville,** or BHV, as it's known. The first street on your left, rue de la Verrerie, will take you down to rue St-Martin and the church of **St-Merri,** an ornate mid-16th-century structure. Its dark interior can be fun to explore, though it contains nothing of outstanding interest. You may find the upscale stores, restaurants, and galleries of rue St-Martin more diverting.

The **Beaubourg/Pompidou Center** or, to give it its full name, the Centre National d'Art et de Culture Georges-Pompidou, is next. Georges Pompidou (1911–1974) was the president of France who inaugurated the project. If nothing else, the Beaubourg is an exuberant melting pot of culture, which casts its net far and wide: Anything goes here. The center hosts an innovative and challenging series of exhibits, in addition to housing the largest collection of modern art in the world. Unveiled in 1977, the Beaubourg is by far the most popular museum in the world, attracting upward of 8 million visitors a year; but it has begun to show its age in no uncertain terms.

You'll approach the center across **plateau Beaubourg,** a substantial square that slopes gently down toward the main entrance. In summer, it's thronged with musicians, mime artists, dancers, fire-eaters, acrobats, and other performers. Probably the single most popular thing to do at the Beaubourg is to ride the escalator up to the roof, with the Parisian skyline unfolding as you are carried through its clear plastic piping. There is a sizable restaurant and café on the roof. The major highlight inside is the modern art collection on the fourth floor. The emphasis is largely on French artists. Movie buffs will want to take in the cinémathèque, a movie theater showing near-continuous programs of classic films from the world over. The bookshop on the first floor stocks a wide range of art books, many in English, plus postcards and posters.

Beaubourg, plateau Beaubourg, tel. 42–77–12– 33. Admission free. Admission to art museum: 28 frs, 32 frs for special exhibitions in the Grande Galerie. Open Wed.–Mon. noon–10 PM, weekends 10 AM–10 PM; closed Tues. Guided tours in English weekdays 3:30, weekends 11 during summer and Christmas seasons only.

6 Take rue Rambuteau, which runs along the north side of the center (to your left as you face the building). The **Quartier de l'Horloge,** the Clock Quarter, opens off the plateau here. An entire city block has been rebuilt, and, though its shops and cafés make a brave attempt to bring it to life, it retains a resolutely artificial quality. The mechanical clock around the corner on rue Clairvaux will amuse kids, however.

Around the Marais

You are now poised to plunge into the elegant heart of the Marais. You won't be able to get into many of the historic homes here—the private hôtels particuliers—but this won't stop you from admiring their stately facades. And don't be afraid to push through the heavy formal doors—or *porte-cochères*—to glimpse the discreet courtyards that lurk behind them.

7 From the Clock Quarter, continue down rue Rambuteau and take the first left, up rue du Temple, to the **Hôtel d'Avaux** at no. 71, built in 1640. The immense entrance is decorated with the sculpted heads of what, in 17th-century France, passed for savages. A few doors up, at **8** no. 79, is the **Hôtel de Montmor,** dating from the same period. It was once the scene of an influential literary salon—a part-social and part-literary group—that met here on an impromptu basis and included the philosopher Descartes (1596–1650) and the playwright Molière (1622–1673). Note the intricate ironwork on the second-floor balcony.

9 Head east on rue des Haudriettes to the little-known **Musée de la Chasse et de la Nature,** housed in one of the Marais's most stately mansions, the Hôtel de Guénégaud. The collections include a series of immense 17th- and 18th-century pictures of dead animals, artfully arranged, as well as a wide variety of guns and stuffed animals. *60 rue des Archives, tel. 42–72–86–43. Admission: 25 frs adults, 5 frs. children under 16. Open Wed.–Mon. 10–12:30 and 1:30–5:30.*

Next door, at 58 rue des Archives, two fairytale towers stand on either side of the Gothic entrance (1380) to the **Hôtel de Clisson.** In the mid-15th century this was the Paris base of the Duke of Bedford, regent of France after Henry V's demise, during the English occupation of Paris, a phase of the Hundred Years War that lasted from 1420 to 1435. At the end of the 17th century, it was bought by the glamorous princess of Soubise, a grande dame of Parisian literary society. She later moved into the neighboring Hôtel de Soubise, now the **Archives Nationales.** Its collections today form part of the **Musée de l'Histoire de France,** whose entrance is at the southern end of the Archives Nationales.

Continue east on rue des Francs-Burgeois, turning left onto rue Vielle du Temple and passing the Hôtel de Rohan (on your left, on the corner), built for the archbishop of Strasbourg in 1705. Turn right onto rue de la Perle and walk down to the **Musée de la Serrure,** the Lock Museum. It's sometimes also called the **Musée Bricard,** a name you'll recognize on many French locks and keys. The sumptuous building in which the collections are housed is perhaps more interesting than the assembled locks and keys within; it was built in 1685 by Bruand, the architect of Les Invalides *(see* From Orsay to Trocadéro, *below).* But those with a taste for fine craftsmanship will appreciate the intricacy and ingenuity of many of the older locks. One represents an early security system—it would shoot anyone who tried to open it with the wrong key. *1 rue de la Perle, tel. 42–77–79–62. Admission: 10 frs. Open Mon.–Fri. 2–5; closed Sat., Sun., Aug., and last week of Dec.*

From here it is but a step to the Hôtel Salé, today the **Musée Picasso,** opened in the fall of 1985 and so far showing no signs of losing its immense popularity. Be prepared for long lines at any time of year. What's notable about the collection—other than the fact that it's the largest collection of works by Picasso in the world—is that these were works that Picasso himself owned; works, in other words, that he especially valued. There are pictures from every period of his life, adding up to a grand total of 230 paintings, 1,500 drawings, and nearly 1,700 prints, as well as works by Cézanne, Miró, Renoir, Braque, Degas, Matisse, and others. If you have any serious interest in Picasso, this is not a place you'd want to miss. The positively palatial surroundings of the Hôtel Salé add greatly to the pleasures of a visit. *5 rue de Thorigny, tel. 42-71-25-21. Admission: 26 frs. Open Thurs.-Mon. 9:30-6.*

Head back down rue de Thorigny and cross to rue Elzévir, opposite. Halfway down on the left **⑭** is the **Musée Cognacq-Jay,** opened here in 1990 after being transferred from its original home on boulevard des Capucines near the Opéra. The museum is devoted to the arts of the 18th century and contains outstanding furniture, porcelain, and paintings (notably by Watteau, Boucher, and Tiepolo). *8 rue Elzévir, tel. 40-27-07-21. Admission: 12 frs, 6 frs students and children. Open Tues.-Sun. 10-5:30.*

Continue down rue Elzévir to **rue des Francs-Bourgeois.** Its name—Street of the Free Citizens—comes from the homes for the poor, or almshouses, built here in the 14th century, whose inhabitants were so impoverished that they were allowed to be "free" of taxes. In marked contrast to the street's earlier poverty, **⑮** the substantial **Hôtel Carnavalet** became the scene, in the late 17th century, of the most brilliant salon in Paris, presided over by Madame de Sévigné. She is best known for the hundreds of letters she wrote to her daughter during her life; they've become one of the most enduring chronicles of French high society in the 17th century, and the Carnavalet was her home for the last 20 years of her life. In 1880, the hotel was transformed into the **Musée Carnavalet,** or Musée Historique de la Ville de Paris. As part of the mammoth celebrations for the bicentennial of the French Revolution, in July 1989, the mu **⑯** seum annexed the neighboring **Hôtel Peletier St-Fargeau.** Together the two museums chronicle the entire history of the city of Paris, with material dating from the city's origins until 1789 housed in the Hôtel Carnavalet, and objects from that time to the present in the Hôtel Peletier St-Fargeau. Parts of the older collections are quite interesting, albeit repetitive. There are large numbers of maps and plans, quantities of furniture, and a substantial assemblage of busts and portraits of Parisian worthies down the ages. The sections on the Revolution, on the other hand, are extraordinary and include some riveting models of guillotines. *23 rue de Sévigné, tel. 42-72-21-13. Admission: 40 frs adults, 30 frs students and senior citizens. Open Tues.-Sun. 10-5:30; closed Mon.*

Now walk a minute or two farther along rue des Francs-Bourgeois to **place des Vosges.** Place des Vosges, or place Royale as it was originally known, is the oldest square in Paris. Laid out by Henri IV at the beginning of the 17th century, it is the model on which all later city squares, that most French of urban developments, are based. The combination of symmetrical town houses and the trim green square, bisected in the center by gravel paths and edged with plane trees, makes place des Vosges one of the more pleasant places to spend a hot summer's afternoon in the city. On these days, it will usually be filled with children playing in shafts of sunlight, with the roar of the traffic a distant hum.

You can tour the **Maison de Victor Hugo** at no. 6 (admission 12 frs, 6.50 frs students; open Tues.-Sun. 10-5:40), where the French author lived between 1832 and 1848. The collections here may appeal only to those with a specialized knowledge of the workaholic French writer.

Around the Bastille

From place des Vosges, follow rue de Pas de la Mule and turn right down boulevard Beaumarchais until you reach **place de la Bastille,** site of the infamous prison destroyed at the beginning of the French Revolution. Until 1988, there was little more to see at place de la Bastille than a huge traffic circle and the **Colonne de Juillet,** the July Column. As part of the country-wide celebrations for July 1989, the bicentennial of the French Revolution, an **opera house** (Opéra de la Bastille) was put up on the south side of the square. Designed by Argentinian-born Carlos Ott, it seats more than 3,000 and boasts five moving stages. This ambitious project has inspired substantial redevelopment on the surrounding streets, especially along rue de Lappe—once a haunt of Edith Piaf—and rue de la Roquette.

The Bastille, or, more properly, the Bastille St-Antoine, was a massive building, protected by eight immense towers and a wide moat (its ground plan is marked by paving stones set into the modern square). It was built by Charles V in the late 14th century. He intended it not as a prison but as a fortress to guard the eastern entrance to the city. By the reign of Louis XIII (1610–1643), however, the Bastille was used almost exclusively to house political prisoners. Voltaire, the Marquis de Sade, and the mysterious Man in the Iron Mask were all incarcerated here, along with many other unfortunates. It was this obviously political role—specifically, the fact that the prisoners were nearly always held by order of the king—that led to the formation of the "furious mob" (in all probability no more than a largely unarmed rabble) to break into the prison on July 14, 1789, to kill the governor, steal what firearms they could find, and set free the seven remaining prisoners.

Toward the Ile St-Louis

There's more of the Marais to be visited between place de la Bastille and the Ile St-Louis, the last leg of this tour. Take wide rue St-Antoine to the **Hôtel de Sully,** site of the **Caisse Nationale des Monuments Historiques,** the principal office for the administration of French historic monuments. Guided visits to sites and buildings all across the city begin here, though all of them are for French-speakers only. Still, it's worth stopping here to look at the stately 17th-century courtyard with its richly carved windows and lavish ornamentation. The bookshop just inside the gate has a wide range of publications on Paris, many of them in English (open daily 10–12:45 and 1:45–6). You can also wander around the gardens.

Those with a fondness for the Baroque should duck into the early 17th-century church of **St-Paul-St-Louis,** a few blocks west on rue St-Antoine. Its abundant decoration, which would be easier to appreciate if the church were cleaned, is typical of the Baroque taste for opulent detail.

The **Hôtel de Beauvais,** located on rue François Miron, is a Renaissance-era hôtel particulier dating from 1655. It was built for one Pierre de Beauvais and financed largely by a series of discreet payments from the king, Louis XIV. These surprisingly generous payments—the Sun King was normally parsimonious toward courtiers—were de Beauvais's reward for having turned a blind eye to the activities of his wife, Catherine-Henriette Bellier, in educating the young monarch in matters sexual. Louis, who came to the throne in 1643 at the age of 4, was 14 at the time Catherine-Henriette gave him the benefit of her wide experience; she was 40.

Continue down rue François Miron. Just before the Hôtel de Ville is the site of one of the first churches in Paris, **St-Gervais- St-Protais,** named after two Roman soldiers martyred by the Emperor Nero in the 1st century. The original church—no trace remains of it now—was built in the 7th century. The present church, a riot of Flamboyant-style decoration, went up between 1494 and 1598, making it one of the last Gothic constructions in the country. Some find this sort of late Gothic architecture a poor, almost degraded, relation of the pure styles of the 12th and 13th centuries. Does it carry off a certain exuberance, or is it simply a mass of unnecessary decoration? You'll want to decide for yourself. Pause before you go in, to look at the facade, put up between 1616 and 1621. Where the interior is late Gothic, the exterior is one of the earliest examples of classical, or Renaissance, style in France. It's also the earliest example of French architects' use of the classical orders of decoration on the capitals (topmost sections) of the columns. Those on the first floor are plain and sturdy Doric; the more elaborate Ionic is used on the second floor; while the most ornate of all—Corinthian—is used on the third floor. The church hosts occasional organ and choral concerts. *Tel. 47-26-78-38 for concert information. Open Tues.-Sun. 6:30 AM-8 PM; closed Mon.*

Don't cross the Seine to Ile St-Louis yet: Take rue de l'Hôtel de Ville to where it meets rue de Figuier. The painstakingly restored **Hôtel de Sens** (1474) on the corner is one of a handful of Parisian homes to have survived since the Middle Ages. With its pointed corner towers, Gothic porch, and richly carved decorative details, it is a strange mixture, half defensive stronghold, half fairytale château. It was built at the end of the 15th century for the archbishop of Sens. Later, its best-known occupants were Henri IV and his queen, Marguerite, philanderers both. Today the building houses a fine arts library, the **Bibliothèque Forney** (admission free; open Tues.-Fri. 1:30-8:30, Sat. 10-8:30).

The Ile St-Louis

Cross pont Marie to the **Ile St-Louis,** the smaller of the two islands in the heart of Paris, linked to the Ile de la Cité by pont St-Louis. The contrast between the islands is striking, considering how close they are. Whereas the Ile de la Cité, the oldest continuously inhabited part of the city, is steeped in history and dotted with dignified, old buildings, the Ile St-Louis is a discreet residential district, something of an extension of the Marais. Once thought to be an unimportant backwater and an area curiously out-of-sync with the rest of the city, Ile St-Louis is now a highly desirable address.

The most striking feature of the island is its architectural unity, which stems from the efforts of a group of early 17th-century property speculators. At that time, there were two islands here, the Ile Notre Dame and Ile aux Vaches—the cows' island, a reference to its use as grazing land. The speculators, led by an energetic engineer named Christophe Marie (after whom the pont Marie was named), bought the two islands, joined them together, and divided the newly formed Ile St-Louis into building plots. Louis Le Vau (1612-1670), the leading Baroque architect in France, was commissioned to put up a series of imposing town houses, and by 1664 the project was largely complete.

There are three things you'll want to do here. One is to walk along **rue St-Louis en l'Ile,** which runs the length of the island. People still talk about its quaint, village-street feel, although this village street is now lined with a high-powered array of designer boutiques and a constant throng of tourists patrolling its length.

Time Out **Berthillon** has become a byword for amazing ice cream. Cafés all over Ile St-Louis sell its glamorous products, but the place to come is still the little shop on rue St-Louis en l'Ile. Expect to wait in line. *31 rue St-Louis en l'Ile. Closed Mon. and Tues.*

The second place to visit is the **Hôtel de Lauzun.** It was built in about 1650 for Charles Gruyn, who accumulated an immense fortune as a supplier of goods to the French army, but who landed in jail before the house was even completed. In the 19th century, the revolutionary critic and visionary poet Charles Baudelaire (1821–1867) had an apartment here, where he kept a personal cache of stuffed snakes and crocodiles. In 1848, the poet Théophile Gautier (1811–1872) moved in, making it the meeting place of the Club des Haschischines, the Hashish-Eaters' Club. Now the building is used for receptions by the mayor of Paris. *17 quai d'Anjou, tel. 43-54-27-14. Admission: 22 frs. Open Easter–Oct., weekends only 10–5:30.*

The third and most popular attraction is a walk along the quays. The most lively, **quai de Bourbon,** is at the western end, facing the Ile de la Cité. There are views of Notre Dame from here and of the Hôtel de Ville and church of St-Gervais-St-Protais on the Right Bank. It can be an almost eerie spot in the winter, when it becomes deserted. In the summer, rows of baking bodies attest to its enduring popularity as the city's favorite sunbathing spot.

From the Arc de Triomphe to the Opéra

Numbers in the margin correspond to points of interest on the Arc de Triomphe to the Opéra map.

This tour takes in grand, opulent Paris: the Paris of imposing vistas, long, arrow-straight streets, and plush hotels and jewelers. It begins at the Arc de Triomphe, standing foursquare at the top of the most famous street in the city, the Champs-Elysées. You'll want to explore both its commercial upper half and its verdant lower section. The hinterland of the Champs-Elysées, made up of the imposing streets leading off it, is equally stylish. You're within striking distance of the Seine here (and a ride on a Bateau-Mouche) to the south, and the cheerful, crowded Faubourg St-Honoré to the north. This is not so much an area for museums as for window-shopping and monument-gazing. Dazzling vistas open up from place de la Concorde, place de la Madeleine, and L'Etoile.

Local charm is not, however, a feature of this exclusive sector of western Paris, occupying principally the 8th Arrondissement. It's beautiful and rich—and a little impersonal. Visit during the day, and head elsewhere in search of Parisian *ambience* and an affordable meal in the evening.

The Arc de Triomphe and Champs-Elysées

Place Charles de Gaulle is known by Parisians as **L'Etoile,** the star—a reference to the streets that fan out from it. It is one of Europe's most chaotic traffic circles, and short of a death-defying dash, your only way of getting to the Arc de Triomphe in the middle is to take an underground passage from the Champs-Elysées or avenue de la Grande Armée.

❶ The colossal, 164-foot **Arc de Triomphe** was planned by Napoléon—who believed himself to

The Arc de Triomphe to the Opéra

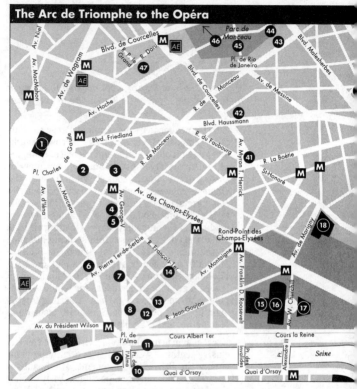

American Cathedral of the Holy Trinity, **7**

Arc de Triomphe, **1**

Atelier de Gustave Moreau, **37**

Bateaux-Mouches, **11**

Crazy Horse Saloon, **8**

Crillon, **26**

Eglise de la Madeleine, **20**

Fauchon, **22**

Galeries Lafayette, **33**

Gare St-Lazare, **38**

George V, **5**

Grand Palais, **16**

Hédiard, **23**

Jardin des Tuileries, **29**

Les Egouts, **10**

Lido, **3**

Maison de la Vigne et du Vin de France, **14**

Marks & Spencer, **35**

Maxim's, **24**

Musée Cernuschi, **44**

Musée de l'Orangerie, **28**

Musée du Jeu de Paume, **27**

Musée Jacquemart-André, **42**

Musée Jean-Jacques Henner, **46**

Musée Nissim de Camondo, **43**

Olympia, **31**

Opéra, **32**

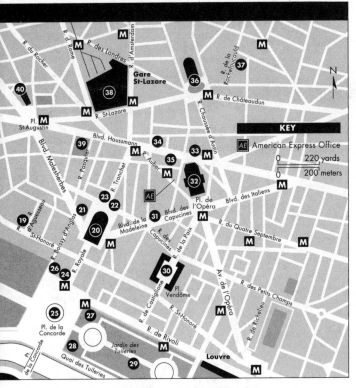

be the direct heir to the Roman emperors—to celebrate his military successes. Unfortunately, Napoléon's strategic and architectural visions were not entirely on the same plane, and the Arc de Triomphe proved something of a white elephant. When it was required for the triumphal entry of his new empress, Marie-Louise, into Paris in 1810, it was still only a few feet high. To save face, a dummy arch of painted canvas was put up.

The view from the top illustrates the star effect of Etoile's 12 radiating avenues and enables you to admire the vista down the Champs-Elysées toward place de la Concorde and the distant Louvre. In the other direction, you can see down avenue de la Grande Armée toward La Tête Défense and its severe modern arch, surrounded by imposing glass and concrete towers. There is a small museum halfway up the arch devoted to its history. France's Unknown Soldier is buried beneath the archway; the flame is rekindled every evening at 6:30. *Pl. Charles-de-Gaulle. Admission: 31 frs adults, 17 frs students and senior citizens, 6 frs children. Open daily 10–5:30, 10–5 in winter. Closed public holidays.*

The cosmopolitan pulse of Paris beats strongest on the gracefully sloping, 1¼-mile-long **Champs-Elysées**. It was originally laid out in the 1660s by the landscape gardener Le Nôtre as a garden sweeping away from the Tuileries, but you will see few signs of these pastoral origins as you stroll past the cafés, restaurants, airline offices, car showrooms, movie theaters, and chic arcades that occupy its upper half.

2 Start off by stopping in at the main **Paris Tourist Office** at no. 127. It's at the Arc de Triomphe end of the Champs-Elysées, on the right-hand side as you arrive from Etoile. It is an invaluable source of information on accommodations, places to visit, and entertainment—both in Paris and in the surrounding Ile-de-France region. *Open daily 9–8, 9–9 on weekdays in summer, 9–6 on Sun. out of season.*

The Champs-Elysées occupies a central role in French national celebrations. It witnesses the finish of the Tour de France bicycle race on the last Sunday of July. It is also the site of vast ceremonies on July 14, France's national, or Bastille, day, and November 11, Armistice Day. Its trees are often decked with the French *tricolore* and foreign flags to mark visits from heads of state.

❸ Three hundred yards down on the left, at 116b, is the famous **Lido** nightclub: Foot-stomping melodies in French and English and champagne-soaked, topless razzmatazz pack in the crowds every night. In contrast are the red-**❹** awninged **Prince de Galles** (Prince of Wales) and **❺** the blue-awninged **George V**, two of the city's top hotels on avenue George-V, a right-hand turn off Champs-Elysées. Continue down avenue George-V, and turn right down Pierre Ier-de-Serbie to the church of **St-Pierre de Chaillot** **❻** on avenue Marceau. The monumental frieze above the entrance, depicting scenes from the life of St. Peter, is the work of Henri Bouchard and dates from 1937.

Returning to avenue George-V, continue toward the slender spire of the **American Cathe-** **❼** **dral of the Holy Trinity,** built by G. S. Street between 1885 and 1888. *Open weekdays 9–12:30 and 2–5, Sat. 9–noon. Services: weekdays 9 AM, Sun. 9 AM and 11 AM; Sun. school and nursery. Guided tours Sun. and Wed. 12:30.*

Continue down to the bottom of the avenue, **❽** passing the **Crazy Horse Saloon** at no. 12, one of Paris's most enduring and spectacular nightspots, to place de l'Alma and the Seine.

❾ The **pont de l'Alma** (Alma bridge) is best known for the chunky stone "Zouave" statue carved into one of the pillars. Zouaves were Algerian infantrymen recruited into the French army who were famous for their bravura and colorful uniforms. Parisians use him to judge the level of the Seine during heavy rains.

Just across the Alma bridge, on the left, is the **❿** entrance to **Les Egouts,** the Paris sewers (admission: 25 frs adults, 20 frs students and senior citizens; open Sat.–Wed. 11–5). Brave the unpleasant—though tolerable—smell and follow the underground passages and footbridges along the sewers' banks. Signs note the streets above you, and detailed panels and displays illuminate the history of waste disposal in Paris, which boasts the second largest sewer system in the world (after Chicago's). If you prefer a less malodorous tour of the city, stay on the Right Bank and head down the sloping side road to the left of the bridge, for the embarkation point of the ⑪ **Bateaux-Mouches.** These popular motorboats set off every half hour, heading east to the Ile St-Louis and then back west, past the Eiffel Tower, as far as the Allée des Cygnes and its miniature version of the Statue of Liberty.

Stylish avenue Montaigne leads from the Seine back toward the Champs-Elysées. The newly ⑫ cleaned facade of the **Théâtre des Champs-Elysées** is a forerunner of the Art Deco style. The theater dates from 1913 and was the first major building in France to be constructed in reinforced concrete. *15 av. Montaigne.*

⑬ A few buildings along is the **Plaza Athénée** hotel (the "Plaza"), a favorite hangout for the *beau monde* who frequent the neighboring haute couture houses. Around the corner on the rue ⑭ François-Ier is the **Maison de la Vigne et du Vin de France.** This is the classy central headquarters of the French wine industry and a useful source of information about wine regions. Bottles and maps are on display. *21 rue François-Ier, tel. 47–20–20–76. Admission free. Open weekdays 9–12:30 and 1:30–6.*

Double back on rue François-Ier as far as Place François-Ier, then turn left onto rue Jean-Goujon, which leads to avenue Franklin D. Roosevelt, another spacious boulevard between Champs-Elysées and the river. Halfway down it ⑮ is the entrance to the **Palais de la Découverte** (Palace of Discovery), whose scientific and technological exhibits include working models and a planetarium. *Av. Franklin-D-Roosevelt. Admission: 21 frs adults, 11 frs children under 18 (15 frs/10 frs extra for planetarium). Open Tues.–Sat. 9:30–6, Sun. 10–7.*

This "Palace of Discovery" occupies the rear half ⑯ of the **Grand Palais.** With its curved glass roof, the Grand Palais is unmistakable when approached from either the Seine or the Champs-

Elysées and forms an attractive duo with the **Petit Palais** on the other side of avenue Winston Churchill. Both these stone buildings, adorned with mosaics and sculpted friezes, seem robust and venerable. In fact, they were erected with indecent haste prior to the Paris World Fair of 1900. Today, the atmospheric iron and glass interior of the Grand Palais plays regular host to major exhibitions. Admire the view from the palaces across the Alexandre III bridge toward the Hôtel des Invalides. *Av. Winston Churchill. Admission varies according to exhibition. Usually open daily 10:30–6:30, and often until 10 PM Wed.*

❶ The **Petit Palais** has a beautifully presented permanent collection of French painting and furniture, with splendid canvases by Courbet and Bouguereau. Temporary exhibits are often held here, too. The sprawling entrance gallery contains several enormous turn-of-the-century paintings on its walls and ceilings. *Av. Winston Churchill. Admission: 12 frs adults, 6 frs children. Open Tues.–Sun. 10–5:30.*

From the Rond-Point des Champs-Elysées, head down avenue de Marigny to rue du Faubourg St-Honoré, a prestigious address in the world of luxury fashion and art galleries. You'll soon spot plenty of both, but may be perplexed at the presence of crash barriers and stern policemen. Their mission: to protect the French **❶** president in the **Palais de l'Elysée.** This "palace," where the head of state lives, works, and receives official visitors, was originally constructed as a private mansion in 1718. Although you catch a glimpse of the palace forecourt and facade through the Faubourg St-Honoré gateway, it is difficult to get much idea of the building's size or of the extensive gardens that stretch back to the Champs-Elysées. The French government—the Conseil des Ministres—attends to more public affairs when it meets here each Wednesday morning. *Not open to the public.*

Toward place de la Concorde

❶ **St. Michael's English Church,** close to the British Embassy on rue du Faubourg St-Honoré, is a modern building whose ugliness is redeemed by the warmth of the welcome afforded to all visitors, English-speaking ones in particular. *5 rue d'Aguesseau, tel. 47–42–70–88. Services Thurs. 12:45 and Sun. 10:30 (with Sunday school) and 6:30; supervised nursery for younger children in the morning.*

Continue down rue du Faubourg St-Honoré to rue Royale. This classy street, lined with jewelry stores, links place de la Concorde to the

⓴ **Eglise de la Madeleine** (closed Sun. 1:30–3:30), a sturdy neo-Classical edifice that was nearly selected as Paris's first train station (the site of what is now the Gare St-Lazare, just up the road, was eventually chosen). With its rows of uncompromising columns, the Madeleine looks more like a Greek temple than a Christian church. Inside, the only natural light comes from three shallow domes. The walls are richly and harmoniously decorated, and gold glints through the murk. The church was designed in 1814 but not consecrated until 1842. The portico's majestic Corinthian colonnade supports a gigantic pediment with a sculptured frieze of the Last Judgment. From the top of the steps, you can admire the view down rue Royale across place de la Concorde to the Palais Bourbon. From the bottom of the steps, another view leads up boulevard Malesherbes to the dome of the church of St-Augustin.

Alongside the Madeleine, between the church
⓵ and L'Ecluse, is a **ticket kiosk** (open Tues.–Sat. 12:30–8) selling tickets for same-day theater performances at greatly reduced prices. Behind
⓶ ⓷ the church are **Fauchon** and **Hédiard,** two stylish delicatessens that are the ultimate in posh nosh. At the end of the rue Royale, just before place
⓸ de la Concorde, is the legendary **Maxim's** restaurant. Unless you choose to eat here—an expensive and not always rewarding experience—you won't be able to see the interior decor, a riot of crimson velvets and florid Art Nouveau furniture.

There is a striking contrast between the sunless, locked-in feel of the high-walled rue Royale
⓹ and the broad, airy **place de la Concorde.** This

huge square is best approached from the Champs-Elysées: The flower beds, chestnut trees, and sandy sidewalks of the avenue's lower section are reminders of its original leafy elegance. Place de la Concorde was built in the 1770s, but there was nothing in the way of peace or concord about its early years. Between 1793 and 1795, it was the scene of over a thousand deaths by guillotine; victims included Louis XVI, Marie Antoinette, Danton, and Robespierre. The obelisk, a present from the viceroy of Egypt, was erected in 1833. The handsome, symmetrical, 18th-century buildings facing the square include the deluxe hotel **Crillon,** though there's nothing so vulgar as a sign to identify it—just an inscribed marble plaque above the doorway.

Facing one side of place de la Concorde are the **Tuileries Gardens.** Two smallish buildings stand sentinel here. To the left, nearer rue de Rivoli, is the **Musée du Jeu de Paume,** fondly known to many as the former home of the Impressionists (now in the Musée d'Orsay). After extensive renovation, the Jeu de Paume reopened in 1991 as a home to brash temporary exhibits of contemporary art. *Admission: 30 frs adults, 20 frs students and senior citizens. Open Tues. noon–9:30, Wed.–Fri. 12–7, weekends 10–7.* The other, identical building, nearer the Seine, is the recently restored **Musée de l'Orangerie,** containing some early 20th-century paintings by Monet (including his vast, eight-paneled *Water Lilies*), Renoir, and other Impressionists. *Place de la Concorde. Admission: 26 frs adults, 14 frs students and senior citizens. Open Wed.–Mon. 9:45–5:15; closed Tues.*

As gardens go, the **Jardin des Tuileries** is typically French: formal and neatly patterned, with statues, rows of trees, gravel paths, and occasional patches of grass trying to look like lawns. These may benefit from the overhaul ordered by Culture Minister Jack Lang for the early '90s. It is a charming place to stroll and survey the surrounding cityscape. To the north is the disciplined, arcaded rue de Rivoli; to the south, the Seine and the gold-hued Musée d'Orsay with its enormous clocks; to the west, the Champs-Elysées and Arc de Triomphe; to the east, the

Arc du Carrousel and the Louvre, with its glass pyramid.

Place Vendôme and the Opéra

30 **Place Vendôme,** north of the Jardin des Tuileries, is one of the world's most opulent squares. Mansart's rhythmic, perfectly proportioned example of 17th-century urban architecture has shone in all its golden-stoned splendor since being cleaned a few years ago. Many other things shine here, too—in jewelers' display windows and on the dresses of guests of the top-ranking **Ritz** hotel. Napoléon had the square's central column made from the melted bronze of 1,200 cannons captured at the battle of Austerlitz in 1805. That's him standing vigilantly at the top. Painter Gustave Courbet headed the Revolutionary hooligans who, in 1871, toppled the column and shattered it into thousands of metallic pieces.

Cross the square and take rue des Capucines on your left to boulevard des Capucines. The **31** **Olympia** music hall is still going strong, though it has lost some of the luster it acquired as the stage for such great postwar singers as Edith Piaf and Jacques Brel.

Time Out There are few grander cafés in Paris than the **Café de la Paix,** on the corner of place de l'Opéra. This is a good place to people-watch, or just to slow down; but expect the prices to be as grand as the setting.

32 The **Opéra,** begun in 1862 by Charles Garnier at the behest of Napoléon III, was not completed until 1875, five years after the emperor's political demise. It is often said to typify the Second Empire style of architecture, which is to say that it is a pompous hodgepodge of styles, imbued with as much subtlety as a Wagnerian cymbal crash. After paying the entry fee, you can stroll around at leisure. The monumental foyer and staircase are boisterously impressive, a stage in their own right, where, on first nights, celebrities preen and prance. If the lavishly upholstered auditorium (ceiling painted by Marc Chagall in 1964) seems small, it is only because the stage is the largest in the world—over

11,000 square yards, with room for up to 450 performers. *Admission: 28 frs, 15 frs children. Open daily 10–4:30, but closed occasionally for rehearsals; call 47–42–57–50 to check.*

Around the Opéra

Behind the Opéra are the *grands magasins*, Paris's most renowned department stores. The nearer of the two, the **Galeries Lafayette,** is the most outstanding, if only because of its vast, shimmering, turn-of-the-century glass dome.

(33)

The domes at the corners of **Printemps,** farther along boulevard Haussmann, to the left, can be best appreciated from the outside; there is a splendid view from the store's rooftop cafeteria.

(34)

Marks & Spencer, across the road, provides a brave outpost for British goods, such as ginger biscuits, bacon rashers, and Cheddar cheese.

(35)

The **Trinité** church, several blocks north of the Opéra, is not an unworthy 19th-century effort at neo-Renaissance style. Its central tower is of dubious aesthetic merit but is a recognizable feature in the Paris skyline (especially since its cleaning in 1986). The church was built in the 1860s and is fronted by a pleasant garden.

(36)

The nearby **Atelier de Gustave Moreau** was the town house and studio of painter Gustave Moreau (1826–1898), doyen of the Symbolist movement that strove to convey ideas through images. Many of the ideas Moreau was trying to express remain obscure to the general public, even though the artist provided explanatory texts. But most onlookers will be content admiring his extravagant colors and flights of fantasy, which reveal the influence of Persian and Indian miniatures. Fantastic details cover every inch of his canvases, and his canvases cover every inch of wall space, making a trip to the museum one of the strangest artistic experiences in Paris. Go on a sunny day, if possible; the low lighting can strain the eyes even more than Moreau's paintings can. *14 rue de la Rochefoucauld. Admission: 17 frs adults, 10 frs children and senior citizens. Open Thurs.–Sun. 10–12:45 and 2–5:15, Mon. and Wed. 11–5:15.*

(37)

Rue St-Lazare leads from Trinité to the **Gare St-Lazare,** whose imposing 19th-century facade

(38)

has been restored. In the days of steam and smoke, the station was an inspiration to several Impressionist painters, notably Monet. Note an eccentric sculpture to the right of the facade—a higgledy-piggledy accumulation of clocks.

39 The leafy, intimate **Square Louis XVI,** off boulevard Haussmann between St-Lazare and St-Augustin, is perhaps the nearest Paris gets to a verdant, London-style square—if you discount the bombastic mausoleum in the middle. The unkempt chapel marks the initial burial site of Louis XVI and Marie Antoinette after their turns at the guillotine on place de la Concorde. Two stone tablets are inscribed with the last missives of the doomed royals—touching pleas for their Revolutionary enemies to be forgiven. *Open daily 10–noon and 2–6, 10–4 in winter.*

Before leaving the square, take a look at the gleaming 1930s-style facade of the bank at the lower corner of rue Pasquier. It has some amusing stone carvings halfway up, representing various exotic animals.

40 A mighty dome is the most striking feature of the innovative iron-and-stone church of **St-Augustin,** dexterously constructed in the 1860s within the confines of an awkward, V-shaped site. The use of metal girders obviated the need for exterior buttressing. The dome is bulky but well-proportioned and contains some grimy but competent frescoes by the popular 19th-century French artist William Bouguereau.

41 Rue La Boétie leads to another church, **St-Philippe du Roule,** built by Chalgrin between 1769 and 1784. Its austere classical portico dominates a busy square. The best thing inside this dimly lit church is the 19th-century fresco above the altar by Théodore Chassériau, featuring the Descent from the Cross.

42 Make your way back to boulevard Haussmann via avenue Myron T. Herrick. The **Musée Jacquemart-André** features Italian Renaissance and 18th-century art in a dazzlingly furnished, late 19th-century mansion. *158 blvd. Haussmann, tel. 42–89–04–91. Admission: 18 frs. Open Wed.–Sun. 1–6.*

Rue de Courcelles and a right on rue de Monceau will lead to place de Rio de Janeiro. Before venturing into the Parc Monceau at the far end of avenue Ruysdaël, continue along rue de Monceau to the **Musée Nissim de Camondo.** Inside, you will find the stylish interior of an aristocratic Parisian mansion in the style of Louis XVI, dating from the last days of the regal Ancien Régime. *63 rue de Monceau. Admission: 18 frs adults, 12 frs students and senior citizens. Open Wed.–Sun. 10–noon and 2–5.*

Rue de Monceau and boulevard Malesherbes lead to the **Musée Cernuschi,** whose collection of Chinese art ranges from neolithic pottery (3rd century BC) to funeral statuary, painted 8th-century silks, and contemporary paintings. *7 av. Velasquez. Admission: 12 frs. Open Tues.–Sun. 10–5:40.*

The **Parc Monceau,** which can be entered from avenue Velasquez, was laid out as a private park in 1778 and retains some of the fanciful elements then in vogue, including mock ruins and a phony pyramid. In 1797, Garnerin, the world's first-recorded parachutist, staged a landing in the park. The rotunda, known as the Chartres Pavilion, was originally a tollhouse and has well-worked iron gates.

Leave the Parc Monceau by these gates and follow rue Phalsbourg and avenue de Villiers to the **Musée Jean-Jacques Henner.** Henner (1829–1905), a nearly forgotten Alsatian artist, here receives a sumptuous tribute. His obsessive fondness for milky-skinned, auburn-haired female nudes is displayed in hundreds of drawings and paintings on the three floors of this gracious museum. *43 av. de Villiers. Admission: 14 frs. Open Tues.–Sun. 10–noon and 2–5.*

Boulevard de Courcelles, which runs along the north side of the Parc Monceau, leads west to rue Pierre-le-Grand (Peter the Great Street). At the far end of that street, at 12 rue Daru, loom the unlikely gilt onion domes of the Russian Orthodox cathedral of **St-Alexandre Nevsky,** erected in neo-Byzantine style in 1860. Inside, the wall of icons that divides the church in two creates an atmosphere seldom found in Roman Catholic or Protestant churches.

From Orsay to Trocadéro

Numbers in the margin correspond to points of interest on the Orsay to Trocadéro map.

The Left Bank has two faces: the cozy, ramshackle Latin Quarter (*see* The Left Bank, *below*) and the spacious, stately 7th Arrondissement. This tour covers the latter, then heads back across the Seine for a look at the museums and attractions clustered around the place du Trocadéro. The latest addition to the area is already the most popular: the Musée d'Orsay. Crowds flock to this stylishly converted train station to see the Impressionists, but also discover important examples of other schools of 19th- and early 20th-century art.

The atmosphere of the 7th Arrondissement is set by the National Assembly, down the river from Orsay, opposite place de la Concorde. French deputies meet here to hammer out laws and insult each other. They resume more civilized attitudes when they return to the luxurious ministries that dot the nearby streets. The most famous is the Hôtel Matignon, official residence of the French prime minister.

The majestic scale of many of the area's buildings is totally in character with the daddy of them all, the Invalides. Like the Champ de Mars nearby, the esplanade in front of the Invalides was once used as a parade ground for Napoléon's troops. In a coffin beneath the Invalides dome, M. Bonaparte dreams on.

Musée d'Orsay

❶ The **Musée d'Orsay** opened in December 1986. It is devoted to the arts (mainly French) produced between 1848 and 1914, and its collections are intended to form a bridge between the classical collections of the Louvre and the modern collections of the Beaubourg. The building began in 1900 as a train station for routes between Paris and the southwest of France. By 1939, the Gare d'Orsay had become too small for mainline travel, and intercity trains were transferred to the

Gare d'Austerlitz. Gare d'Orsay became a suburban terminus until, in the 1960s, it closed for good. After various temporary uses (a theater and auction house among them), the building was set for demolition. However, the destruction of the 19th-century Les Halles (market halls) across the Seine provoked a furor among conservationists, and in the late 1970s, President Giscard d'Estaing, with an eye firmly on establishing his place in the annals of French culture, ordered Orsay to be transformed into a museum. The architects Pierre Colboc, Renaud Bardou, and Jean-Paul Philippon were commissioned to remodel the building, while Gae Aulenti, known for her renovation of the Palazzo Grassi in Venice, was hired to redesign the interior.

The chief artistic attraction is the Impressionists, whose works are displayed on the top floor, next to the museum café. Renoir, Sisley, Pissarro, and Monet are all well represented. Highlights for many visitors are Monet's *Poppy Field* and Renoir's *Le Moulin de la Galette*. The Post-Impressionists—Cézanne, van Gogh, Gauguin, and Toulouse-Lautrec—are all also represented on this floor.

On the first floor, you'll find the work of Manet and the delicate nuances of Degas. Pride of place, at least in art historical terms, goes to Manet's *Déjeuner sur l'Herbe*, the painting that scandalized Paris in 1863. Another reworking by Manet of a classical motif is his reclining nude, *Olympia*. Gazing boldly out from the canvas, she was more than respectable 19th-century Parisian proprieties could stand.

Those who prefer more correct academic paintings should look at Puvis de Chavannes's larger-than-life classical canvases. The pale, limpid beauty of his figures is enjoying considerable attention after years of neglect. Those who are excited by more modern developments will make for the early 20th-century Fauves (meaning wild beasts, the name given them by an outraged critic in 1905)—particularly Matisse, Derain, and Vlaminck.

Orsay to Trocadéro

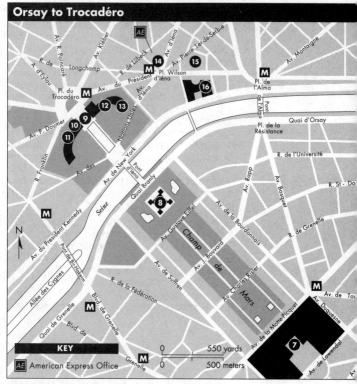

KEY

AE American Express Office

0 — 550 yards
0 — 500 meters

Ecole Militaire, **7**

Eiffel Tower, **8**

Hôtel des Invalides, **6**

Hôtel Matignon, **4**

Musée d'Art Moderne de la Ville de Paris, **16**

Musée de la Légion d'Honneur, **2**

Musée de la Marine, **11**

Musée de l'Homme, **10**

Musée des Monuments Français, **12**

Musée d'Orsay, **1**

Musée du Cinéma, **13**

Musée Guimet, **14**

Musée Rodin, **5**

Palais Bourbon, **3**

Palais de Chaillot, **9**

Palais Galliera, **15**

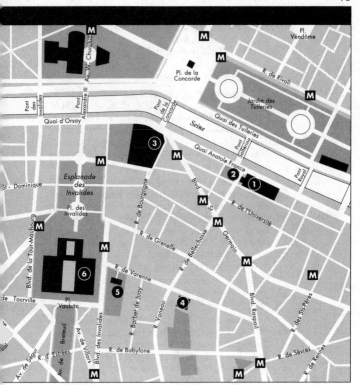

Sculpture at the Orsay means, first and foremost, Rodin (though there's more to enjoy at the Musée Rodin, *see below*). Two further highlights are the faithfully restored BelleEpoque restaurant and the model of the entire Opéra quarter, displayed beneath a glass floor.

The Musée d'Orsay, otherwise known as M.O., is already one of Paris's star attractions. Crowds are smaller at lunchtime and on Thursday evenings. *1 rue de Bellechasse. Admission: 31 frs adults, 16 frs students and senior citizens and on Sun. Open Tues.–Sat. 10–6, Thurs. 10–9:30, and Sun. 9–6.*

Across from the Musée d'Orsay stands the
② **Musée de la Légion d'Honneur.** French and foreign decorations are displayed in this stylish mansion by the Seine (officially known as the Hôtel de Salm). The original building, constructed in 1786, burned during the Commune in 1871 and was rebuilt in 1878. *2 rue de Bellechasse. Admission: 10 frs. Open Tues.–Sun. 2–5.*

Toward the Invalides

Continue along the left bank of the Seine to the
③ 18th-century **Palais Bourbon** (directly across from place de la Concorde), home of the Assemblée Nationale (French Parliament). The colonnaded facade, commissioned by Napoléon, is a sparkling sight after a recent cleaning program. There is a fine view from the steps across to place de la Concorde and the church of the Madeleine. *Not open to the public.*

The quiet, distinguished 18th-century streets behind the Palais Bourbon are filled with embassies and ministries. The most famous, reached via rue de Bourgogne and rue de
④ Varenne, is the **Hôtel Matignon,** residence of the French Prime Minister, and Left Bank counterpart to the President's Elysée Palace. "Matignon" was built in 1721 but has housed heads of government only since 1958. From 1888 to 1914, it was the embassy of the Austro-Hungarian Empire. *57 rue de Varenne. Neither house nor garden is open to the public.*

Another glorious town house along rue de Varenne is the Hôtel Biron, better known as the **⑤ Musée Rodin.** The splendid house, with its spacious vestibule, broad staircase, and light, airy rooms, retains much of its 18th-century atmosphere and makes a handsome setting for the sculpture of Auguste Rodin (1840–1917). You'll doubtless recognize the seated *Thinker (Le Penseur)*, with his elbow resting on his knee, and the passionate *Kiss.* There is also an outstanding white marble bust of Austrian composer *Gustav Mahler*, as well as numerous examples of Rodin's obsession with hands and erotic subjects.

The second-floor rooms, which contain some fine paintings by Rodin's friend Eugène Carrière (1849–1906), afford views of the large garden behind the house. Don't go without visiting the garden: It is exceptional both for its rose bushes (over 2,000 of them, representing 100 varieties) and for its sculpture, including a powerful statue of the novelist Balzac and the despairing group of medieval city fathers known as the *Burghers of Calais. 77 rue de Varenne. Admission: 21 frs, 10 frs Sun. Open Easter–Oct., Tues.–Sun. 10–6; Nov.–Easter, Tues.–Sun. 10–5.*

⑥ From the Rodin Museum, you can see the **Hôtel des Invalides,** along rue de Varenne. It was founded by Louis XIV in 1674 to house wounded (or "invalid") veterans. Although no more than a handful of old soldiers live at the Invalides today, the military link remains in the form of the **Musée de l'Armée**—one of the world's foremost military museums—with a vast collection of arms, armor, uniforms, banners, and military pictures down through the ages.

The **Musée des Plans-Reliefs,** housed on the fifth floor of the right-hand wing, contains a fascinating collection of scale models of French towns made to illustrate the fortifications planned by Vauban in the 17th century. (Vauban was a superb military engineer who worked under Louis XIV.) The largest and most impressive is Strasbourg, which takes up an entire room. Not all of Vauban's models are here, however. As part of a cultural decentralization program, France's so-

cialist government of the early 1980s decided to
pack the models (which had languished for years
in dusty neglect) off to Lille in northern France.
Only half the models had been shifted when a
conservative government returned to office in
1986 and called for their return. Ex-Prime Minister Pierre Mauroy, the socialist mayor of Lille,
refused, however, and the impasse seems set to
continue.

The museums are not the only reason for visiting the Invalides. The building itself is an
outstanding monumental ensemble in late-
17th-century Baroque, designed by Bruand and
Mansart. The main, cobbled courtyard is a fit-
ting scene for the parades and ceremonies still
occasionally held here. The most impressive
dome in Paris towers over the **Eglise du Dôme**
(church of the Dome). Before stopping here,
however, visit the 17th-century **Eglise St-Louis
des Invalides,** the Invalides's original church,
and the site of the first performance of Berlioz's
Requiem in 1837.

The Dôme church was built onto the end of
Eglise St-Louis but was blocked off from it in
1793—no great pity perhaps, as the two buildings are vastly different in style and scale. It
was designed by Mansart and built between
1677 and 1735. The remains of Napoléon are
here, in a series of no fewer than six coffins, one
inside the next, within a bombastic tomb of red
porphyry, ringed by low reliefs and a dozen statues symbolizing Napoléon's campaigns. Among
others commemorated in the church are French
World War I hero Marshal Foch; Napoléon's
brother Joseph, erstwhile king of Spain; and
fortification-builder Vauban, whose heart was
brought to the Invalides at Napoléon's behest.
*Hôtel des Invalides. Admission: 32 frs adults,
20 frs children. Open daily 10–6; 10–5 in winter. A son-et-lumière (sound-and-light) show in
English is held in the main courtyard on evenings throughout the summer.*

Cross the pleasant lawns outside the Dôme
church to place Vauban. Follow avenue de
Tourville to the right, and turn left onto avenue
de la Motte-Picquet.

The Eiffel Tower and the Trocadéro

A few minutes' walk will bring you face-to-face with the Eiffel Tower. Spare a thought for the **Ecole Militaire** on your left; it is 18th-century architecture at its most harmonious. It is still in use as a military academy and therefore not open to the public.

The pleasant expanse of the **Champ de Mars** makes an ideal approach to the **Eiffel Tower**, whose colossal bulk (it's far bigger and sturdier than pictures suggest) becomes evident the nearer you get. It was built by Gustave Eiffel for the World Exhibition of 1889, the centennial of the French Revolution, and was still in good shape to celebrate its own 100th birthday. Recent restoration hasn't made the elevators any faster (lines are inevitable), but the new nocturnal illumination is fantastic—every girder highlighted in glorious detail.

Such was Eiffel's engineering wizardry that even in the strongest winds his tower never sways more than 4½ inches. Today, it is Paris's best-known landmark and exudes a feeling of permanence. As you stand beneath its huge legs, you may have trouble believing that it nearly became 7,000 tons of scrap-iron when its concession expired in 1909. Only its potential use as a radio antenna saved the day; it now bristles with a forest of radio and television transmitters. If you're full of energy, stride up the stairs as far as the third deck. If you want to go to the top, you'll have to take the elevator. The view at 1,000 feet may not beat that from the Tour Maine-Montparnasse (*see* The Left Bank, *below*), but the setting makes it considerably more romantic. *Pont d'Iéna. Cost by elevator: 2nd floor, 17 frs; 3rd floor, 34 frs; 4th floor, 51 frs. Cost by foot: 8 frs (2nd and 3rd floors only). Open July–Aug., daily 9 AM–midnight; Sept.– June, daily 9:30 AM–11 PM.*

Just across the Pont d'Iena from the Eiffel Tower, on the heights of Trocadéro, is the muscular, sandy-colored **Palais de Chaillot**—a cultural center built in the 1930s to replace a Moorish-style building constructed for the World Exhibition of 1878. The gardens between the Palais de Chaillot and the Seine contain an aquarium and some dramatic fountains. The terrace between the two wings of the palace offers a wonderful view of the Eiffel Tower.

The Palais de Chaillot contains four large museums, two in each wing. In the left wing (as you approach from the Seine) are the Musée de l'Homme and the Musée de la Marine. The

🔟 **Musée de l'Homme,** on the second and third floors, is an earnest anthropological museum with primitive and prehistoric artifacts from throughout the world. *Admission: 25 frs adults, 15 frs children. Open Wed.–Mon. 9:45–5.* The

⑪ **Musée de la Marine,** on the first floor, is a maritime museum with a salty collection of ship models and seafaring paraphernalia, illustrating French naval history right up to the age of the nuclear submarine. *Admission: 28 frs adults, 14 frs senior citizens, students, and children. Open Wed.–Mon. 10–6.*

⑫ The other wing is dominated by the **Musée des Monuments Français,** without question the best introduction to French medieval architecture. This extraordinary museum was founded in 1879 by architect-restorer Viollet-le-Duc (the man who more than anyone was responsible for the extensive renovation of Notre Dame). It pays tribute to French buildings, mainly of the Romanesque and Gothic periods (roughly 1000–1500), in the form of painstaking copies of statues, columns, archways, and frescoes. It is easy to imagine yourself strolling among ruins as you pass through the first-floor gallery. Substantial sections of a number of French churches and cathedrals are represented here, notably Chartres and Vézelay. Mural and ceiling paintings—copies of works in churches around the country—dominate the other three floors. The value of these paintings has become increasingly evident as many of the originals continue to deteriorate. On the ceiling of a circular room is a reproduction of the painted dome of Cahors cathedral, giving the visitor a more vivid sense of the skills of the original medieval painter than the cathedral itself. *Admission: 16 frs, 8 frs on Sun. Open Wed.–Mon. 9:45–5:15.*

⑬ The **Musée du Cinéma,** located in the basement of this wing, traces the history of motion pictures since the 1880s. *Admission: 22 frs. Open Wed.–Mon. Guided tours only, at 10, 11, 2, 3, and 4.*

The area around the Palais de Chaillot offers a
(14) feast for museum lovers. The **Musée Guimet** (down avenue du Président Wilson, at place d'Iéna) has three floors of Indo-Chinese and Far Eastern art, initially amassed by 19th-century collector Emile Guimet. Among the museum's bewildering variety of exhibits are stone buddhas, Chinese bronzes, ceramics, and painted screens. *6 pl. d'Iéna. Admission: 26 frs adults, 14 frs students and senior citizens. Open Wed.–Mon. 9:45–5:15.*

Some 200 yards down avenue Pierre-Ier-de-
(15) Serbie is the **Palais Galliera,** home of the small and some would say overpriced Museum of Fashion and Costume. This stylish, late-19th-century town house hosts revolving exhibits of costume, design, and accessories, usually based on a single theme. *10 av. Pierre-Ier-de-Serbie. Admission: 25 frs adults, 15 frs students and senior citizens. Open Tues.–Sun. 10–5:40.*

(16) The **Musée d'Art Moderne de la Ville de Paris** has both temporary exhibits and a permanent collection of modern art, continuing where the Musée d'Orsay leaves off. Among the earliest works are Fauvist paintings by Vlaminck and Derain, followed by Picasso's early experiments in Cubism. No other Paris museum exudes such a feeling of space and light. Its vast, unobtrusive, white-walled galleries provide an ideal background for the bold statements of 20th-century art. Loudest and largest are the canvases of Robert Delaunay. Other highlights include works by Braque, Rouault, Gleizes, Da Silva, Gromaire, and Modigliani. There is an excellent bookshop specializing in 19th- and 20th-century art and architecture, with many books in English. *11 av. du Président Wilson. Admission: 15 frs, half-price on Sun. for permanent exhibitions only. Open Tues.–Sun. 10–5:30, Wed. 10–8:30.*

The Left Bank

Numbers in the margin correspond to points of interest on the Left Bank map.

References to the Left Bank have never lost their power to evoke the most piquant of all images of Paris. Although the bohemian strain the area once nurtured has lost much of its vigor, people who choose it today as a place to live or work are, in effect, turning their backs on the formality and staidness of the Right Bank.

The Latin Quarter is the geographic and cerebral hub of the Left Bank, populated mainly by Sorbonne students and academics who fill the air of the cafés with their ideas—and their tobacco smoke. (The university began as a theological school in the Middle Ages and later became the headquarters of the University of Paris; in 1968, the student revolution here had an explosive effect on French politics, resulting in major reforms in the education system.) The name Latin Quarter comes from the university tradition of studying and speaking in Latin, a tradition that disappeared during the Revolution.

St-Michel to St-Germain

❶ **Place St-Michel** is a good starting point for exploring the rich slice of Parisian life, from its most ancient to its most modern, that the Left Bank offers. Leave your itineraries at home, and wander along the neighboring streets lined with restaurants, cafés, galleries, old bookshops, and all sorts of clothing stores, from tiny boutiques to haute couture showrooms.

For a route crowded more with humanity and less with car and bus traffic, pick up the pedestrian rue St-André des Arts at the southwest corner of place St-Michel. **Studio St-André des Arts,** at no. 30, is one of Paris's most popular experimental cinemas. Just before you reach the Carrefour de Buci crossroads at the end of the street, turn onto the **Cour du Commerce St-André.** Jean-Paul Marat printed his revolutionary newspaper, *L'Ami du Peuple,* at no. 8; and it was here that Dr. Guillotin conceived the idea for a new, "humane" method of execution that was used during the Revolution—it was rumored that he practiced it on sheep first—and that remained the means of executing convicted criminals in France until President Mitterrand abolished it in 1981.

Down a small passageway on the left stands one of the few remaining towers of the 12th-century fortress wall built by Philippe-Auguste. The ❹ passage leads you to the **Cour de Rohan,** a series of three cloistered courtyards that were part of the hôtel of the archbishops of Rouen, established in the 15th century; the name has been corrupted over the years to Rohan.

Rejoin the Cour du Commerce St-André and ❺ continue to the **Carrefour de Buci,** once a notorious Left Bank landmark. By the 18th century, it contained a gallows, an execution stake, and an iron collar for punishing troublemakers. In September 1792, the Revolutionary army used this daunting site to enroll its first volunteers, and many Royalists and priests lost their heads here during the bloody course of the Revolution. There's nothing sinister, however, about the Carrefour today. Brightly colored flowers spill onto the sidewalk at the **Grange à Buci** flower shop, on the corner of rue Grégoire-de-Tours. ❻ **Rue de Buci** has one of the best markets in Paris. *Open Tues.–Sun. till 1 PM.*

Several interesting, smaller streets of some historical significance radiate from the Carrefour. ❼ **Rue de l'Ancienne-Comédie,** which cuts through to the busy place de l'Odéon, is so named because it was the first home of the now legendary French theater company, the Comédie Française. The street was named in 1770, the very year the Comédie left for the Tuileries palace. The company moved again later to the Odéon, before heading to its present home by the Palais-Royal (*see* The Historic Heart, *above*).

Across the street from the company's first home ❽ (no. 14) is the oldest café in Paris, **Le Procope.** Opened in 1686 by an Italian named Francesco Procopio (only three years before the Odéon itself opened), it has been a watering hole for many of Paris's most famous literary sons and daughters over the centuries; Diderot, Voltaire,

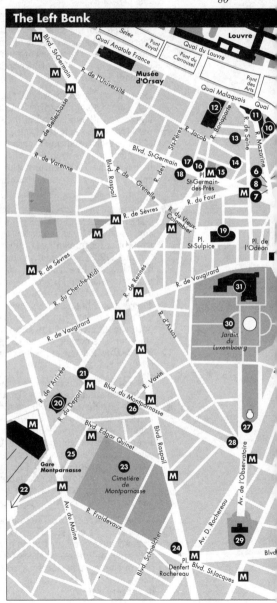

The Left Bank

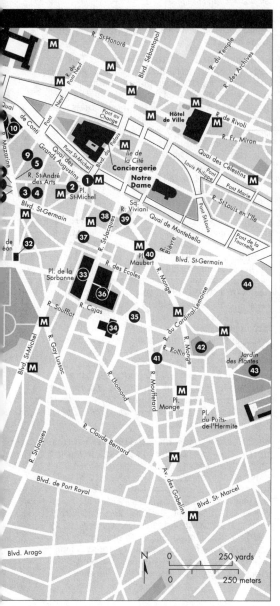

Balzac, George Sand, Victor Hugo, and Oscar Wilde were some of its more famous and infamous regulars.

Stretching north from the Carrefour de Buci toward the Seine is the **rue Dauphine,** the street that singer Juliet Greco put on the map when she opened the Tabou jazz club here in the '50s. It attracted a group of young intellectuals who were to become known as the Zazous, a St-Germain movement promoting the jazz culture, complete with all-night parties and free love. The cult author Boris Vian liked to play his trumpet through the night, an activity that did little to endear him to the club's neighbors. You may still find jazz played here, but the club is a shadow of its former self.

The next street that shoots out of the Carrefour (moving counterclockwise) is rue Mazarine. Here stands the **Hôtel des Monnaies,** the national mint. Louis XVI transferred the Royal Mint to this imposing mansion in the late 18th century. Although the mint was moved to Pessac, near Bordeaux, in 1973, weights and measures, medals, and limited-edition coins are still made here. In June 1988, an enlarged **Musée Monétaire** opened so that the vast collection of coins, documents, engravings, and paintings could be displayed. The workshops are on the second floor. On Tuesday and Friday afternoons you'll catch the coin and medal craftsmen at work; their ateliers overlook the Seine. *11 quai de Conti. Admission: 20 frs adults, 15 frs students and senior citizens. 15 frs Sun. Open Tues., Thurs.–Sun. 1–6, Wed. 1–9.*

Next door is the **Institut de France.** With its distinctive dome and commanding position over the quai at the foot of the Pont des Arts, it is not only one of France's most revered cultural institutions but also one of the Left Bank's most impressive waterside sights. The **Académie Française,** the oldest of the five academies that comprise the Institut de France, was created by Cardinal Richelieu in 1635. Its first major task was to edit the French dictionary; today, among other functions, it is still charged with safeguarding the purity of the French language.

Spend your
vacation
touring
castles.
Not train
stations.

Vacation Cars. Vacation Prices. Wherever your destination in Europe, there is sure to be one of more than 1,000 Budget locations nearby. Budget offers considerable values on a wide variety of quality cars, and if you book before you leave the U.S., you'll save even more with a special rate package from the Budget World Travel Plan. For information and reservations, contact your travel consultant or call Budget in the U.S. at **800-472-3325.** Or, while traveling abroad, call a Budget reservation center.

THE SMART MONEY IS ON BUDGET.

We feature Ford and other fine cars.   *A system of corporate and licensee owned locations.*

Just west along the waterfront, on quai Mala-
quais, stands the **Ecole Nationale des Beaux-
Arts,** whose students can usually be seen painting and sketching on the nearby quais and
bridges. The school—today the breeding
ground for France's foremost painters, sculptors, and architects—was once the site of a convent, founded in 1608 by Marguerite de Valois,
the first wife of Henri IV. During the Revolution, the convent was turned into a depot for
works of art salvaged from the monuments that
were under threat of destruction by impas-
sioned mobs. Only the church and cloister remained, however, when the Beaux-Arts school
was established in 1816. Allow yourself time to
wander into the courtyard and galleries of the
school to see the casts and copies of the statues
that were once stored here, or stop in at one of
the temporary exhibitions of professors' and
students' works. *14 rue Bonaparte. Open daily
1–7.*

Tiny **rue Visconti,** running east–west off rue Bonaparte (across from the entrance to the Beaux-
Arts), has a lot of history packed into its short
length. In the 16th century, it was known as
Paris's Little Geneva—named after Europe's
foremost Protestant city—because of the Protestant ghetto that formed here. Racine, one of
France's greatest playwrights and tragic poets,
lived at no. 24 until his death in 1699. Balzac set
up a printing shop at no. 17 in 1826, and the fiery
Romantic artist Eugène Delacroix (1798–1863)
worked here from 1836 to 1844.

Time Out The terrace at **La Palette** (43 rue de Seine) beckons as soon as you reach the rue de Seine, at the
end of rue Visconti. This popular café has long
been a favorite haunt of Beaux Arts students.
One of them was allowed to paint an ungainly
portrait of the *patron*, François, which presides
with mock authority over the shaggy gathering
of clients.

Swing right at the next corner onto the pretty
rue Jacob, where both Wagner and Stendhal
once lived. Follow rue Jacob across rue des
Saints-Pères, where it changes to rue de l'Université. You are now in the Carré Rive Gauche,

the Left Bank's concentrated quarter-mile of art dealers and galleries.

Return on rue Jacob until you are almost back to rue de Seine. Take the rue de Fürstemberg to the quiet place Fürstemberg, bedecked with white globe lamps and catalpa trees. Here is **Atelier Delacroix,** Delacroix's former studio, containing only a paltry collection of sketches and drawings by the artist; the garden at the rear of the studio is almost as interesting. Nonetheless, those who feel the need to pay homage to France's foremost Romantic painter will want to make the pilgrimage. *Place Fürstemberg. Admission: 12 frs adults, 7 frs ages 18–25 and over 60, 7 frs on Sun. Open Wed.–Mon. 9:45–5:15.*

St-Germain-des-Prés, Paris's oldest church, began as a shelter for a relic of the True Cross brought back from Spain in AD 542. Behind it, rue de l'Abbaye runs alongside the former Abbey palace, dating from AD 990 and once part of a powerful Benedictine abbey. The chancel was enlarged and the church then consecrated by Pope Alexander III in 1163. Interesting interior details include the colorful 19th-century frescoes in the nave by Hippolyte Flandrin, a pupil of the classical painter Ingres, depicting vivid scenes from the Old Testament. The church stages superb organ concerts and recitals; programs are displayed outside and in the weekly periodicals *Officiel des Spectacles* and *Pariscope. Open weekdays 8–7:30; weekends 8–9.*

Across the cobbled place St-Germain-des-Prés stands the celebrated **Les Deux Magots** café, named after the grotesque Chinese figures, or *magots,* inside. It still thrives on its post–World War II reputation as one of the Left Bank's prime meeting places for the intelligentsia. Though the Deux Magots remains crowded day and night, these days, you're more likely to rub shoulders with tourists than with philosophers.

In the postwar years, Jean-Paul Sartre and Simone de Beauvoir would meet "the family" two doors down at the **Café de Flore** on boulevard St-Germain. "The family" was de Beauvoir's name for their close-knit group, which included fellow-graduates from the prestigious

Ecole Normale Supérieure and writers from Gaston Gallimard's publishing house in the nearby rue Sébastien-Bottin. Today the Flore has become more of a gay hangout, but, along with the Deux Magots and the pricey **Brasserie Lipp** across the street, where politicians and show-biz types come to wine and dine (after being "passed" by the doorman), it is a scenic spot that never lacks for action.

A large part of the area south of boulevard St-Germain, around rue de Grenelle and rue des Saints-Pères, has undergone enormous change but is still home to publishing houses, bookstores, and galleries.

For contrast, take rue du Vieux-Colombier through the Carrefour de La Croix Rouge to place St-Sulpice. This newly renovated square is ringed with cafés, and Yves St-Laurent's famous Rive Gauche store is at no. 6. Looming over the square is the enormous 17th-century church of **St-Sulpice.** The 18th-century facade was never finished, and its unequal towers add a playful touch to an otherwise sober design. The interior is baldly impersonal, however, despite the magnificent Delacroix frescoes—notably Jacob wrestling with the angel—in the first chapel on your right. If you now pick up the long rue de Rennes and follow it south, you'll soon arrive in the heart of Montparnasse.

Montparnasse

With the growth of Paris as a business and tourist capital, commercialization seems to have filled any area where departing residents and businesses have created a vacuum. Nowhere else is this more true than in and around the vaulting, concrete space and starkly functionalist buildings that have come to rule Montparnasse. Seeing it now, it is difficult to believe that in the years after World War I, Montparnasse replaced Montmartre as *the* place in which Parisian artists came to live.

The opening of the 59-story **Tour Maine-Montparnasse** in 1973 forever changed the face of this painters' and poets' haunt. (The name Montparnasse itself came from some 17th-century students, who christened the area after Mount

Parnassus, the home of Apollo, leader of the Muses.) The tower was part of a vast redevelopment plan that aimed to make the area one of Paris's premier business and shopping districts. Fifty-two floors of the tower are taken up by offices, while a vast commercial complex, including a Galeries Lafayette department store, spreads over the first floor. Although it is uninspiring by day, it becomes a neon-lit beacon for the area at night. As Europe's tallest high rise, it affords stupendous views of Paris; on a clear day, you can see for 30 miles. It also claims to have the fastest elevator in Europe! *Admission: 40 frs adults, 30 frs students and senior citizens, 22 frs children 5–14. Open daily 9:30 AM–10:30 PM, weekdays 10 AM–9:30 PM in winter.*

㉑ Immediately north of the tower is **place du 18 Juin 1940,** part of what was once the old Montparnasse train station and a significant spot in Parisian World War II history. It is named for the date of the radio speech Charles de Gaulle made, from London, urging the French to continue resisting the Germans after the fall of the country to Nazi Germany in May 1940. In August 1944, the German military governor, Dietrich von Choltitz, surrendered to the Allies here, ignoring Hitler's orders to destroy the city as he withdrew; the French General Philippe Leclerc subsequently used it as his headquarters.

Behind the older train station, Gare Montparnasse, you'll see the huge new train terminal that serves Chartres, Versailles, and the west of France. Since 1990, the high-speed *TGV Atlantique* leaves here for Brittany (Rennes and Nantes) and the southwest (Bordeaux, via Tours, Poitiers, and Angoulême). South of this station is one of the oddest residential complexes to appear in this era of architectural ex-

㉒ perimentation. The **Amphithéâtre,** built by Ricardo Boffil, is eye-catching but stark and lacking in human dimension.

㉓ The **Cimetière de Montparnasse** (Montparnasse cemetery) contains many of the quarter's most illustrious residents, buried only a stone's throw away from where they worked and played. It is not at all a picturesque cemetery (with the exception of the old windmill in the corner, which used to be a student tavern) but seeing the names of some of its inhabitants— Baudelaire, Maupassant, Saint-Saëns, and the industrialist André Citroën—may make the visit worthwhile. Nearby, at place Denfert-Rochereau, is the entrance to an extensive complex of **catacombs** (*denfert* is a corruption of the word for hell, *enfer*). The catacombs are stocked with the bones of millions of skeletons that were moved here in 1785 from the area's charnel houses. *Admission: 16 frs adults, 10 frs students and senior citizens. Open Tues.–Fri. 2–4, weekends 9–11 and 2–4.*

Montparnasse's bohemian aura has dwindled to almost nothing, yet the area hops at night as *the* place in Paris to find movies of every description, many of them shown in their original language. Theaters and theater-cafés abound, too, especially along seedy **rue de la Gaîté.** The Gaîté-Montparnasse, Le Théâtre Montparnasse, and Le Grand Edgar are among the most popular. Up boulevard du Montparnasse and across from the Vavin métro station are two of the better-known gathering places of Montparnasse's heyday, the **Dôme** and **La Coupole** brasseries. La Coupole opened in 1927 as a bar/restaurant/dance hall and soon became a home away from home for some of the area's most famous residents, such as Apollinaire, Max Jacob, Cocteau, Satie, Stravinsky, and the ubiquitous Hemingway. It may not be quite the same mecca these days, but it still pulls in a classy crowd.

Across the boulevard, rue Vavin leads past two more celebrated Montparnasse cafés, the **Sélect** and the **Rotonde,** to the Jardin du Luxembourg. But stay on boulevard du Montparnasse for the intersection with boulevard St-Michel, where the verdant **avenue de l'Observatoire** begins its long sweep up to the Luxembourg gardens. Here you'll find perhaps the most famous bastion of the Left Bank café culture, the **Closerie des Lilas.** Now a pricey bar/restaurant, the Closerie remains a staple on all literary tours of Paris not least because of the commemorative plaques fastened onto the bar, marking the places where renowned personages sat. Baudelaire, Verlaine, Hemingway, and Apollinaire are just a few of the names. Although the lilacs *(lilas)* have gone from the terrace, it is still a pretty place, opening onto the luxuriant green of the surrounding parkland, and as crowded in the summer as it ever was in the '30s.

29 The vista from the Closerie includes the **Paris Observatory** (to the right), built in 1667 by Louis XIV. Its four facades were built to align with the four cardinal points—north, south, east, and west—and its southern wall is the determining point for Paris's official latitude, 48° 50′11″N. French time was based on this Paris meridian until 1911, when the country decided to adopt the international Greenwich Meridian.

A tree-lined alley leads along the avenue de l'Observatoire to the gardens, but before the entrance, you'll pass Davioud's **Fontaine de l'Observatoire** (Observatory Fountain), built in 1873 and decked with four statues representing the four quarters of the globe. Look north from here and you'll have a captivating view of Montmartre and Sacré-Coeur, with the gardens in the foreground.

Palais du Luxembourg

30 From avenue de l'Observatoire walk up to the **Jardin du Luxembourg** (the Luxembourg Gardens), one of the city's few large parks. Its fountains, ponds, trim hedges, precisely planted rows of trees, and gravel walks are typical of the French fondness for formal gardens. At the far **31** end is the **Palais du Luxembourg,** gray and imposing, built, like the park, for Maria de' Medici, widow of Henri IV, at the beginning of the 17th century. The palace remained royal property until the Revolution, when the state took it over and used it as a prison. Danton, the painter David, and Thomas Paine were all detained here. Today, it is the site of the French Senate and is not open to the public.

32 The **Théâtre National de l'Odéon,** set at the north end of the Luxembourg Gardens, was established in 1792 to house the Comédiens Français troupe. The massive structure you see today replaced the original theater, which was destroyed by fire in 1807. Since World War II, it has specialized in 20th-century productions. It was the base for Jean-Louis Barrault's and Madeleine Renaud's theater company, the Théâtre de France, until they fell out of favor with the authorities for their alleged role in spurring on the student revolutionaries in May 1968. Today, the Théâtre de l'Odéon is the French home of the Theater of Europe and stages some excellent productions by major foreign companies.

The Sorbonne and the Latin Quarter

If you follow rue de Vaugirard (the longest street in Paris) one block east to boulevard St-Michel, you will soon be at the **place de la Sorbonne,** the hub of the Latin Quarter and nerve center of the student population that has always held such sway over Left Bank life. The square is dominated by the Eglise de la Sorbonne, whose outstanding exterior features are its cupola and 10 Corinthian columns. Inside is the white marble tomb of Cardinal Richelieu. (The church is open to the public only during exhibitions and cultural events.) The university buildings of La Sorbonne spread out around the church from rue Cujas down to the visitor's entrance on rue des Ecoles.

33 The **Sorbonne** is the oldest university in Paris—indeed, one of the oldest in Europe—and has for centuries been one of France's principal institutions of higher learning. It is named after Robert de Sorbon, a medieval canon who founded a theological college here in 1253 for 16 students. By the 17th century, the church and university buildings were becoming dilapidated, so Cardinal Richelieu undertook to have them restored; the present-day Sorbonne campus is largely a result of that restoration. Despite changes in the neighborhood, the maze of amphitheaters, lecture rooms, and laboratories, and the surrounding courtyards and narrow streets, still have a hallowed air. For a glimpse of a more recent relic of Sorbonne history, look for Puvis de Chavannes's painting of the *Sacred Wood* in the main lecture hall, a major meeting point during the tumultuous student upheavals of 1968, and now a university landmark.

Behind the Sorbonne, bordering its eastern reach, is the rue St-Jacques. The street climbs

toward the rue Soufflot, named to honor the
34 man who built the vast, domed **Panthéon,** set
atop place du Panthéon. One of Paris's most
physically overwhelming sites—it was commissioned by Louis XV as a mark of gratitude for
his recovery from a grave illness in 1744—the
Panthéon is now a seldom-used church, with little of interest except for Puvis de Chavannes's
monumental frescoes and the crypt, which holds
the remains of Voltaire, Zola, and Rousseau. In
1789—the year the church was completed—its
windows were blocked by order of the Revolutionary Constituent Assembly, and they have
remained that way ever since, adding to its se-
pulchral gloom. The dome, which weighs about
10,000 tons, is best appreciated from a distance.
*Admission: 25 frs, 14 frs ages 18–25, 6 frs chil-
dren 7–17. Open daily 10–5:30.*

Diagonally across from the Panthéon on the
corner of rue Clovis and rue Cujas stands the
35 striking **St-Etienne-du-Mont.** This mainly 16th-
century church's ornate facade combines Gothic, Baroque, and Renaissance elements. Inside,
the fretted rood screen is the only one of its kind
in Paris. Note the uneven-floored chapel behind
the choir, which can be reached via a cloister
containing some exquisite stained glass dating
from the 17th century.

Up rue St-Jacques again and across from the
Sorbonne are the **Lycée Louis-le-Grand** (Mo-
36 lière, Voltaire, and Robespierre studied here)
and the elite **Collège de France,** whose grounds
continue around the corner onto rue des Ecoles.
In 1530, François I created this school as the
College of Three Languages, which taught High
Latin, Greek, and Hebrew, and any other subjects eschewed by academics at the Sorbonne.
Diagonally across from the college, on the other
side of rue des Ecoles, is the **square Paul-
Painlevé;** behind it lies the entrance to the inimi-
table Hôtel et Musée de Cluny.

Built on the site of the city's enormous old Ro-
37 man baths, the **Musée de Cluny** is housed in a
15th-century mansion that originally belonged
to monks of Cluny Abbey in Burgundy. The remains of the baths that can still be seen are what
survived a sacking by Barbarians in the 4th cen-

tury. But the real reason people come to the Cluny is for its tapestry collection. The most famous series of all is the graceful *Lady and the Unicorn, or Dame à la Licorne,* woven in the 15th or 16th century, probably in the southern Netherlands. And if the tapestries themselves aren't enough at which to marvel, there is also an exhibition of decorative arts from the Middle Ages, a vaulted chapel, and a deep, cloistered courtyard with mullioned windows, set off by the *Boatmen's Pillar,* Paris's oldest sculpture, at its center. *Admission: 17 frs, 9 frs children and Sun. Open Wed.–Mon. 9:30–5:15.*

Above boulevard St-Germain, rue St-Jacques reaches toward the Seine, bringing you past the
38 elegant proportions of the church of **St-Séverin.** Rebuilt in the 16th century and noted for its width and its Flamboyant Gothic style, the church dominates a close-knit Left Bank neighborhood filled with quiet squares and pedestrian streets. Note the splendidly deviant spiraling column in the forest of pillars behind the altar. *Open weekdays 11–5:30, Sat. 11–10.*

Running riot around the relative quiet of St-Séverin are streets filled with restaurants of every description, serving everything from souvlaki-to-go to five-course haute cuisine. There is definitely something for every budget here. Rue de la Huchette is the most heavily trafficked of the restaurant streets and especially good for its selection of cheaper Greek food houses and Tunisian pâtisseries.

Cross to the other side of rue St-Jacques. In Square René Viviani, which surrounds the
39 church of **St-Julien-le-Pauvre,** stands an acacia tree that is supposed to be the oldest tree in Paris (although it has a rival claim from another acacia at the Jardin des Plantes). This tree-filled square also gives you one of the more spectacular views of Notre Dame. The tiny church here was built at the same time as Notre Dame (1165–1220), on a site where a whole succession of chapels once stood. The church belongs to a Greek Orthodox order today, but was originally named for St. Julian, bishop of Le Mans, who was nicknamed "Le Pauvre" after he gave all his money away.

Behind the church, to the east, are the tiny, elegant streets of the recently renovated **Maubert** district, bordered by quai de Montebello and boulevard St-Germain. Rue de Bièvre, once filled with tanneries, is now guarded at both ends to protect President Mitterrand's private residence.

Public meetings and demonstrations have been held in place Maubert ever since the Middle Ages. Nowadays, most gatherings are held inside or in front of the elegantly Art Deco **Palais de la Mutualité,** on the corner of the square, also a venue for jazz, pop, and rock concerts. On Tuesdays, Thursdays, and Saturdays, it is transformed into a colorful outdoor market.

Head up rue Monge, turn right onto rue du Cardinal-Lemoine, and you'll find yourself at the minute **place de la Contrescarpe.** It doesn't start to swing until after dusk, when its cafés and bars fill up. During the day, the square looks almost provincial, as Parisians flock to the daily market on rue Mouffetard. There are restaurants and cafés of every description on rue Mouffetard, and if you get here at lunchtime, you may want to buy yourself the makings for an alfresco lunch and take it to the unconventional picnic spot provided by the nearby Gallo-Roman ruin of the **Arènes de Lutèce;** it begins on rue Monge, just past the end of rue Rollin. The ancient arena was discovered only in 1869 and has since been excavated and landscaped to reveal parts of the original Roman amphitheater. This site and the remains of the baths at the Cluny constitute the only extant evidence of the powerful Roman city of Lutetia that flourished here in the 3rd century. It is also one of the lesser-known delights of the Left Bank, so you are not likely to find it crowded.

The **Jardin des Plantes** is an enormous swath of greenery containing spacious botanical gardens and a number of natural history museums. It is stocked with plants dating back to the first collections here in the 17th century, and has been enhanced ever since by subsequent generations of devoted French botanists. It claims to shelter Paris's oldest tree, an *acacia robinia*, planted in 1636. There is also a small, old-fashioned zoo here; an alpine garden; an aquarium; a maze; and a number of hothouses. The **Musée Entomologique** is devoted to insects; the **Musée Paléontologique** exhibits fossils and prehistoric animals; the **Musée Minéralogique** houses a stupendous collection of rocks and minerals. *Admission: 12–25 frs. Museums open Wed.–Mon. 9–11:45 and 1–4:45, weekends 2–4:45.*

Time Out At the back of the gardens, in place du Puits-de-l'Hermite, you can drink a restorative cup of sweet mint tea in **La Mosquée,** a beautiful white mosque, complete with minaret. Once inside, you'll be convinced that you must be elsewhere than the Left Bank of Paris. The students from the nearby Jussieu and Censier universities pack themselves into the Moslem restaurant here, which serves copious quantities of couscous. The sunken garden and tiled patios are open to the public—the prayer rooms are not—and so are the *hammams,* or Turkish baths. *Baths open daily 11 AM–8 PM; Fri. and Sun. men only; Mon., Wed., Thurs., and Sat. women only. Admission: 15 frs, 65 frs for Turkish baths. Guided tours of mosque Sat.–Thurs. 10–noon and 2–5:30.*

In 1988, Paris's large Arab population gained another base: the huge **Institut du Monde Arabe,** which overlooks the Seine on quai St-Bernard, just beyond Université Jussieu. Jean Nouvel's harmonious mixture of Arabic and European styles was greeted with enthusiasm when the center first opened. Note on the building's south side the 240 shutter-like apertures that open and close to regulate light exposure. It contains a sound and image center, a wall of televisions, with Arab programming, a vast library and a documentation center. *23 quai St-Bernard. Admission free. Open Tues.–Sun. 10–6.*

Montmartre

Numbers in the margin correspond to points of interest on the Montmartre map.

On a dramatic rise above the city is Montmartre, site of the Sacré-Coeur basilica and home to a once-thriving artistic community, a heritage recalled today chiefly by the gangs of third-rate painters clustered in the area's most famous square, the place du Tertre. Despite their presence, and the fact that the fabled nightlife of old Montmartre has fizzled down to some glitzy nightclubs and porn shows, Montmartre still exudes a sense of history, a timeless quality infused with that hard-to-define Gallic charm.

Seeing Montmartre means negotiating a lot of steep streets and flights of steps. If the prospect of trudging up and down them is daunting, you can tour parts of Montmartre by public transportation, aboard the Promotrain or the Montmartrobus. The Promotrain offers daily 40-minute guided tours of Montmartre between 10 AM and midnight. The cost is 25 francs for adults, 15 francs for children under 12, and departures are from outside the Moulin Rouge on place Blanche. The Montmartrobus is a regular city bus that runs around Montmartre for the price of a métro ticket. It departs from place Pigalle. If you're visiting only Sacré-Coeur, take the funicular that runs up the hill to the church near Anvers métro station.

Exploring Montmartre

❶ Begin your tour at **place Blanche,** site of the Moulin Rouge. Place Blanche—White Square—takes its name from the clouds of chalky dust churned up by the windmills that once dotted Montmartre (or *La Butte,* meaning "mound" or "hillock"). They were set up here not just because the hill was a good place to catch the wind—at over 300 feet, it's the highest point in the city—but because Montmartre was covered with wheat fields and quarries right up to the end of the 19th century. The carts carrying away the wheat and crushed stone trundled across place Blanche, turning the square white as they passed. Today, only two of the original 20 windmills are intact. A number have been converted to other uses, none more famous than

❷ the **Moulin Rouge,** or Red Windmill, built in 1885 and turned into a dance hall in 1900. It was a genuinely wild place in its early days, immortalized by Toulouse-Lautrec in his boldly simple posters and paintings. The place is still trading shamelessly on the notion of Paris as a city of

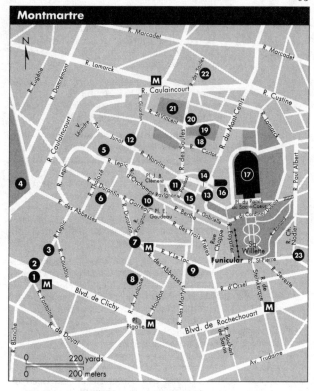

Montmartre

Basilique du Sacré-Coeur, **17**	Lapin Agile, **20**	Place des Abbesses, **7**
Bateau-Lavoir, **10**	Marché St-Pierre, **23**	Place du Tertre, **13**
Chapelle du Martyre, **9**	Moulin de la Galette, **5**	Rue Lepic, **3**
Cimetière de Montmartre, **4**	Moulin de Paris, **11**	St-Pierre de Montmartre, **16**
Cité Internationale des Arts, **12**	Moulin Rouge, **2**	St-Vincent Cemetery, **21**
Espace Dali, **15**	Musée d'Art Juif, **22**	Studio 28, **6**
La Mère Catherine, **14**	Musée du Vieux Montmartre, **18**	Théâtre Libre, **8**
	Place Blanche, **1**	Vineyard, **19**

sin: If you fancy a Vegas-style night out, with computerized light shows and troupes of bare-breasted girls sporting feather headdresses, this is the place to go (*see* The Arts and Nightlife, Chapter 6).

③ For a taste of something more authentically French, walk past the Moulin Rouge, up **rue Lepic,** site of one of the most colorful and tempting food markets in Paris (closed Mon.).

④ Turn left onto rue des Abbesses and walk along to **Cimetière de Montmartre** (Montmartre cemetery). It's by no means as romantic or as large as the better known Père Lachaise cemetery in the east of the city, but it contains the graves of many prominent French men and women, including the 18th-century painters Greuze and Fragonard; Degas; and Adolphe Sax, inventor of the saxophone. The Russian ballet dancer Nijinsky is also buried here.

Walk back along rue des Abbesses. Rue Tholozé, the second street on the left, was once a path over the hill, the oldest in Montmartre. It **⑤** leads to the **Moulin de la Galette,** one of the two remaining windmills in Montmartre, which has been unromantically rebuilt. To reach it, you **⑥** pass **Studio 28.** This seems to be no more than a generic little movie theater, but when opened in 1928, it was the first purposely built *art et essai,* or experimental theater, in the world. Over the years, the movies of directors like Jean Cocteau, François Truffaut, and Orson Welles have often been shown here before their official premieres.

Return to rue des Abbesses, turn left, and walk **⑦** to **place des Abbesses.** The little square is typical of the kind of picturesque and slightly countrified style that has made Montmartre famous. The entrance to the métro station, a curving, sensuous mass of delicate iron, is one of a handful of original Art Nouveau stations left in Paris. The austere, red brick **church of St-Jean l'Evangéliste** (1904) is worth a look, too. It was one of the first concrete buildings in France; the brick had to be added later to soothe offended locals. The **café St-Jean,** next to it, is a popular local meeting place, crowded on weekends.

There are two competing attractions just off the square. Theater buffs should head down the tiny rue André-Antoine. At no. 37, you'll see what **⑧** was originally the **Théâtre Libre,** or Free Theater, founded in 1887 by André Antoine and immensely influential in popularizing the work of iconoclastic young playwrights such as Ibsen and Strindberg. The other attraction is **rue Yvonne-le-Tac,** scene of a vital event in Montmartre's early history and linked to the disputed story of how this quarter got its name. Some say the name Montmartre comes from the Roman temple to Mercury that was once here, called the Mound of Mercury or *Mons Mercurii.* Others contend that it was an adaptation of *Mons Martyrum,* a name inspired by the burial here of Paris's first bishop, St-Denis. The popular version of his martyrdom is that he was beheaded by the Romans in AD 250, but arose to carry his severed head from rue Yvonne-le-Tac to a place 4 miles to the north, an area now known as St-Denis. He is commemorated by the **⑨** 19th-century **Chapelle du Martyre** at no. 9, built over the spot where he is said to have been executed. It was in the crypt of the original chapel here that St. Ignatius of Loyola founded the Jesuit order in 1540, a decisive step in the efforts of the Catholic Church to reassert its authority in the face of the Protestant Reformation.

From rue Yvonne-le-Tac, retrace your steps through place des Abbesses. Take rue Ravignan on the right, climbing to the summit via place Emile-Goudeau, an enchanting little cobbled **⑩** square. Your goal is the **Bateau-Lavoir,** or Boat Wash House, at its northern edge. Montmartre poet Max Jacob coined the name for the old building on this site, which burned down in 1970. First of all, he said, it resembled a boat. Second, the warren of artists' studios within was always cluttered and paint-splattered, and looked to be in perpetual need of a good hosing down. The new building also contains art studios, but, if you didn't know its history, you'd probably walk right past it; it is the epitome of poured concrete drabness. It was in the original Bateau-Lavoir that painters Picasso and Braque, early this century, made their first bold stabs at the concept of Cubism—a move that paved the way for abstract painting.

Continue up the hill to place Jean-Baptiste Clément. The Italian painter and sculptor Modigliani (1884–1920) had a studio here at no. 7. Some have claimed he was the greatest Italian artist of the 20th century, the man who fused the genius of the Italian Renaissance with the modernity of Cézanne and Picasso. He claimed that he would drink himself to death—he eventually did—and chose the right part of town to do it in. This was one of the wildest areas of Montmartre. Its bistros and cabarets have mostly gone now, though, and only the **Moulin de Paris** still reflects a glimmer of the old atmosphere. Look for the octagonal tower at the north end of the square; it's all that's left of Montmartre's first water tower, built around 1840 to boost the area's feeble water supply.

Rue Norvins, formerly rue des Moulins, runs behind and parallel to the north end of the square. Turn left along it to reach stylish avenue Junot, site of the **Cité Internationale des Arts** (International Residence of the Arts), where the city authorities rent out studios to artists from all over the world. Retrace your steps back to rue Norvins and continue east past the bars and tourist shops, until you reach place du Tertre.

Place du Tertre (*tertre* means hillock) regains its village atmosphere only in the winter, when the somber buildings gather in the grays of the Parisian light and the plane tree branches sketch traceries against the sky. At any other time of year, you'll have to fight your way through the crowds to the southern end of the square and the breathtaking view over the city. The real drawback is the swarm of artists clamoring to dash off your portrait. Most are licensed to be there, and, like taxi drivers, their prices are officially fixed. But there is no shortage of con men, sketch pads in hand, who will charge whatever they think they can get away with. If one produces a picture of you without having first asked, you're under no obligation to buy it, though that's not to say you won't have to argue your case. It's best just to walk away.

14 **La Mère Catherine,** the restaurant at the northern end of the square, has an honored place in
French culinary history. It was a favorite with
the Russian cossacks who occupied Paris in 1814
after Napoléon had been exiled to the island of
Elba. Little did they know that when they
banged on the tables and shouted *"bistro,"* the
Russian word for "quick," they were inventing a
new breed of French restaurant. For a restaurant catering almost entirely to the tourist
trade, La Mère Catherine is surprisingly good,
though prices are high for what's offered.

Time Out **Patachou,** opened in 1987, sounds the one classy
note on place du Tertre (at no. 9). It offers exquisite, if expensive, cakes and teas.

15 Around the corner on rue Poulbot, the **Espace
Dali** houses more than 300 works by Salvador
Dali, who once kept a studio in the area. The museum's atmosphere is meant to approximate the
surreal experience, with black walls, low lighting, and a new-agey musical score—punctuated
by recordings of Dali's own voice. If you're interested in seeing some of Dali's less-familiar
works, including a series of sculptures and
bronzes, a visit will prove worthwhile. Those
unmoved by this eccentric genius and showman
may want to skip this stop in favor of strolling
the place du Tertre. *11 rue Poulbot, tel. 42–64–
40–10. Admission: 35 frs adults, 25 frs children. Open daily 10–7; until 8 in summer.*

It was in place du Tertre in March 1871 that one
of the most destructively violent episodes in
French history began, one that colored French
political life for generations. Despite popular
images of later-19th-century France—and Paris especially—as carefree and prosperous, for
much of this period the country was desperately
divided into two camps: an ever more vocal and
militant underclass, motivated by resentment
of what they considered an elitist government,
and a reactionary and fearful bourgeoisie and
ruling class. It was a conflict that went back at
least as far as the French Revolution at the end
of the 18th century, and one that twice flared
into outbreaks of civil war and rebellion, in 1832
and 1848, as the country oscillated between re-

publican and imperial forms of government. In
1870, France, under the leadership of an oppor-
tunistic but feeble Napoléon III (nephew of the
great Napoléon), was drawn into a disastrous
war with Bismarck's Prussia, which was rapidly
growing into one of the most formidable military powers in Europe. (Soon after, Prussia was
to dominate a newly united and aggressive Germany.) In September that year, Prussia in-
vaded France, surrounded Paris, and laid siege
to it. After four months of appalling suffering—
during which time the Louvre became a muni-
tions factory, the Gare de Lyon was converted
into a cannon foundry, and the two elephants in
the zoo, Castor and Pollux, were eaten by starv-
ing Parisians—the new government under
French statesman Adolphe Thiers capitulated.
Although mass starvation seemed imminent,
fears that Thiers would restore an imperial
rather than a republican government caused Parisians to refuse to surrender their arms to him.
Thiers then ordered that the guns at Montmartre be captured by loyal government forces.
Insurgents responded by shooting the two gen-
erals ordered to retake the guns. Almost immediately, barricades were thrown up across the
city streets, and the fighting began in earnest.
The antimonarchists formed the Commune,
which for three heady months ruled Paris. In
May, from his base at Versailles, Thiers ordered
the city retaken. Estimates as to the numbers
killed in the fighting vary greatly. Some say
4,000 Communards lost their lives; others claim
20,000. No one, however, doubts that upward of
10,000 Communards were executed by government troops after the collapse of the Commune.

In expiation for this bloodshed, the French government decided, in 1873 (after the downfall of
Thiers), to build the basilica of the Sacré-Coeur.
It was to be a sort of national guilt offering. Before visiting this landmark, walk to the church
16 of **St-Pierre de Montmartre** at the east side of
place du Tertre. It's one of the oldest churches in
the city, built in the 12th century as the abbey
church of a substantial Benedictine monastery.
It's been remodeled on a number of occasions
down through the years, and the 18th-century
facade, built by Louis XIV, contrasts uncom-

fortably with the mostly medieval interior. Its setting is awkward, too: The bulk of the Sacré-Coeur looms directly behind it.

⑰ The **Basilique du Sacré-Coeur,** begun in 1873 and completed in 1910 (though not consecrated until 1919), symbolized the return of relative self-confidence to later-19th-century Paris after the turmoil of the Commune. Even so, the building was to some extent a reflection of political divisions within the country. It was largely financed by French Catholics fearful of an anticlerical backlash and determined to make a grand statement on behalf of the Church. Stylistically, the Sacré-Coeur borrows elements from Romanesque and Byzantine models, fusing them under its distinctive Oriental dome. Built on a grand scale, the effect is strangely disjointed and unsettling, rather as if the building had been designed by an architect of railway stations, with a pronounced taste for exoticism. The gloomy, cavernous interior is worth visiting for its golden mosaics; climb to the top of the dome for the view over Paris.

More of Montmartre beckons north and west of the Sacré-Coeur. Take rue du Mont-Cenis down **⑱** to rue Cortot, site of the **Musée du Vieux Montmartre.** Like the Bateau-Lavoir, the building that is now the museum sheltered an illustrious group of painters, writers, and assorted cabaret artists in its heyday toward the end of the 19th century. Foremost among them were Renoir—he painted the *Moulin de la Galette,* an archetypical Parisian scene of sun-drenched revels, while he lived here—and Maurice Utrillo, Montmartre painter par excellence. Utrillo was encouraged to paint by his mother, Suzanne Valadon, a regular model of Renoir's and a considerable painter in her own right. Look carefully at the pictures in the museum here and you can see the plaster and sand he mixed with his paints to help convey the decaying buildings of the area. Almost the best thing about the muse- **⑲** um, however, is the view over the tiny **vineyard** on neighboring rue des Saules, the only vineyard in Paris, which still produces a symbolic 125 gallons of wine every year. It's hardly vintage stuff, but there are predictably bacchanalian celebrations during the October harvest.

*Musée du Vieux Montmartre, 12 rue Cortot.
Admission: 25 frs adults, 15 frs students and
senior citizens. Open Tues.–Sun. 11–5:30.*

There's an equally famous Montmartre landmark on the corner of rue St-Vincent, just down
the road: the **Lapin Agile.** It's a bar-cabaret and
originally one of the raunchiest haunts in Montmartre. Today, it manages against all odds to
preserve at least something of its earlier flavor,
unlike the Moulin Rouge. It got its curious
name—it means the Nimble Rabbit—when the
owner, André Gill, hung a sign outside (you can
see it now in the Musée du Vieux Montmartre)
of a laughing rabbit jumping out of a saucepan
clutching a wine bottle. In those days, the place
was still tamely called La Campagne (The Coun-
tryside). Once the sign went up, locals rebap-
tized the place Lapin à Gill, which, translated,
means rabbit, Gill-style. When in 1886 it was
sold to cabaret singer Jules Jouy, he called it the
Lapin Agile, which has the same pronunciation
in French as Lapin à Gill. In 1903, the premises
were bought by the most celebrated cabaret en-
trepreneur of them all, Aristide Bruand, por-
trayed by Toulouse-Lautrec in a series of
famous posters.

Behind the Lapin Agile is the **St-Vincent Cemetery;** the entrance is off little rue Lucien-
Gaulard. It's a tiny graveyard, but serious
students of Montmartre might want to visit to
see Utrillo's burial place.

Continue north on rue des Saules, across busy
rue Caulaincourt, and you come to the **Musée
d'Art Juif,** the Museum of Jewish Art. It contains devotional items, models of synagogues,
and works by Pissarro and Marc Chagall. *42 rue
des Saules. Admission: 20 frs adults, 15 frs students and children. Open Sun.–Thurs. 3–6.*

There are several routes you can take back over
Montmartre's hill. Luxurious avenue Junot,
from which you'll see the villa Léandre, one of
Montmartre's most charming side streets,
makes for a picturesque return from the area
around the cemetery and the museum. Alternatively, you can turn east onto rue Lamarck, past
several good restaurants, to circle around the
quieter side of the Sacré-Coeur basilica. If you

then take the little stairpath named after Utrillo down to rue Paul Albert, you'll come upon the

㉓ **Marché St-Pierre** (St. Pierre Market), the perfect place to rummage for old clothes and fabrics. Prices are low. *Open Tues.–Sun. 8–1.*

Take rue de Steinkerque, opposite the foot of the Sacré-Coeur gardens, then turn right onto boulevard de Rochechouart and continue down to **Place Pigalle** to complete your tour of the essential Montmartre. Despite the area's reputation as a tawdry red-light district, a number of trendy clubs have opened here (*see* The Arts and Nightlife, Chapter 6). If you choose to visit at night, however, be aware that dubious characters and lewd sex shows still prevail.

3 Shopping

By Corinne LaBalme

Corinne LaBalme is a Paris-based freelance writer and a contributing editor for United Airlines' Hemispheres.

Window-shopping is one of Paris's great spectator sports. Tastefully displayed wares—luscious cream-filled éclairs, lacy lingerie, rare artwork, gleaming copper pots—entice the eye and awaken the imagination. And shopping is one of the city's greatest pastimes, a chance to mix with Parisians and feel the heartbeat of the country. Who can understand the magic of French cuisine until they've explored a French open-air produce market on a weekend morning? Or resist the thrill of seeing a Chanel evening gown displayed in its own glossy Paris boutique—where even the doorknobs are shaped like Chanel Number 5 crystal perfume stoppers?

Department Stores

Opéra area   **Au Printemps** (64 blvd. Haussmann, 9e, tel. 42–82–50–00) is a glittery three-store complex that includes "La Maison," for housewares and furniture; "La Mode," for ladies and children; and "Brummel," a six-floor emporium devoted to menswear. *Open Mon.–Sat. 9:30–7.*

Galeries Lafayette (40 blvd. Haussmann, 9e, tel. 42–82–34–56) is equally elegant, and it spices up its Parisian aura with periodic exhibits featuring crafts from exotic countries. Stylish private-label fashions (Briefing and Jodphur) offer good value. *Open Mon–Sat. 9:30–6:45. Another branch is at Centre Commercial Montparnasse, 15e, tel. 45–38–52–87.*

Marks & Spencer (35 blvd. Haussmann, 9e, tel. 47–42–42–91) is a British store chiefly noted for its moderately priced sportswear and its excellent English grocery and take-out food service. *Open Mon.–Sat. 9:30–7, Tues. 10–7.*

Louvre–Pont   La Samaritaine (19 rue de la Monnaie, 1er, tel. **Neuf area**   40–41–20–20), a sprawling four-store complex. Especially good for kitchen supplies, housewares, and furniture, it's famous for its rooftop snackbar that offers a marvelous view of Notre Dame. *Open Mon.–Sat. 9:30–7, Thurs. 9:30–10.*

Hôtel de   Bazar de l'Hôtel de Ville (52–64 rue de Rivoli, **Ville/Marais**   4e, tel. 42–74–90–00). The fashion offerings are **area**   minimal, but BHV is noteworthy for quality

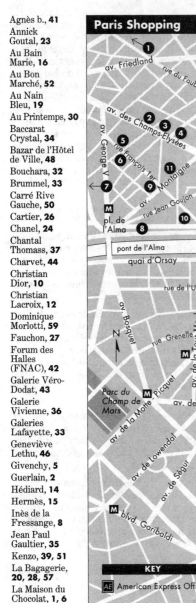
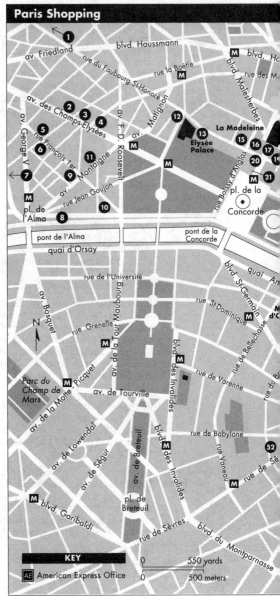

Paris Shopping

La Madeleine

Elysée Palace

pl. de la Concorde

pont de l'Alma

pont de la Concorde

quai d'Orsay

rue de l'Université

rue Grenelle

Parc du Champ de Mars

av. de Tourville

pl. de Breteuil

rue de Babylone

rue de Sèvres

blvd. du Montparnasse

N

KEY

AE American Express Office

| 0 | 550 yards |
| 0 | 500 meters |

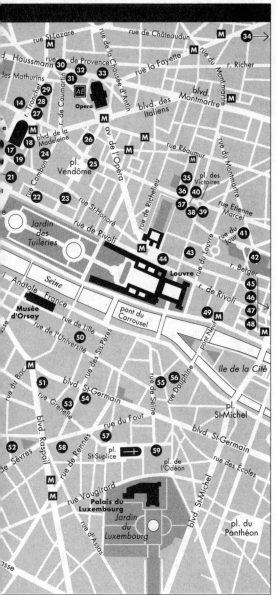

household goods, home decor materials, and office supplies. *Open Mon.–Sat. 9:30–7, Wed. 9:30–10.*

Left Bank **Au Bon Marché** (22 rue de Sèvres, 7e, tel. 44–39–80–00), founded in 1852, is chiefly known for linens, table settings, and high-quality furniture. La Grande Epicerie, a grocery store and deli here, is a gourmet's delight. The basement is a treasure trove for books, records, and arty gifts. *Open Mon.–Fri. 9:30–6:30, Sat. 9:30–7.*

Budget Most Parisians dash into their neighborhood **Monoprix** or **Prisunic** stores—with branches throughout the city—at least once a week. These handy shops stock inexpensive cosmetics, toothpaste, groceries, toys, typing paper, bathmats—a little of everything.

Specialty Shops

Antiques **Louvre des Antiquaires** (2 pl. du Palais-Royal, 1er) is an elegant multifloor complex where 250 of Paris's leading dealers showcase their rarest objects.

Carré Rive Gauche is a compact Left Bank district, bordered by the quai Voltaire and the rue de l'Université, whose narrow sidestreets shelter dozens of fine arts and antiques galleries.

Bags and **La Bagagerie** (41 rue du Four, 6e, tel. 45–48–
Luggage 85–88; also 11 rue du Fbg. St-Honoré, 8e, tel. 47–42–79–13, and 12 rue Tronchet, 8e, tel. 42–65–03–40) features brightly colored bags and belts with youthful style and moderate prices.

Hermès (24 rue du Fbg. St-Honoré, 8e, tel. 40–17–47–17). Its most famous leather creation is the eternally chic Kelly bag, created for Grace Kelly. Prices are astronomical.

Clothing **Chanel** (42 av. Montaigne, 8e, tel. 47–23–74–
(Women's) 12, and 29 rue Cambon, 1er) has undergone a
Classic Chic radical transformation under Karl Lagerfeld, who has added leather 'n' chains to classic suits and accessories.

Christian Dior (30 av. Montaigne, 8e, tel. 40–73–54–44) is a pearl gray palace selling ladies' and menswear, perfumes, jewelry, lingerie, furs, leather goods, porcelain, and gifts.

Givenchy Boutique (8 av. Georges V, 8e, tel. 47–20–81–31) presents slightly more affordable versions of the designer's elegant ready-to-wear.

Nina Ricci (39 av. Montaigne, 8e, tel. 47–23–78–88) clothes are supremely ladylike, and the lingerie is luxuriantly romantic.

Trendsetters **Christian Lacroix** (26 av. Montaigne, 8e, tel. 47–20–68–95, and 73 rue du Fbg. St-Honoré, 8e) turns haute couture into a Provençal carnival with daring cuts and candy-coated colors.

Jean-Paul Gaultier (6 rue Vivienne, 2e, tel. 42–86–05–05), Madonna's clothier, specializes in outrageously attention-getting garments for men and women.

Lolita Lempicka (13 bis rue Pavée, 4e, tel. 42–74–50–48) serves up sharp suits and whimsical silk dresses. Lolita bis, a lower-priced junior line, is sold in a shop across the street.

Romeo Gigli (46 rue de Sévigné, 4e, tel. 48–04–57–05) offers the oversized Renaissance-style clothing for men and women that has bestowed cult status upon this Milan-based designer.

Thierry Mugler (10 pl. des Victoires, 2e, tel. 42–60–06–37, and 49 av. Montaigne, 8e, tel. 47–23–37–62), with kinky lace-up dresses and sexy cat-suits, keeps fans coming back for more—menswear is next door at no. 8.

Chic and **Agnes b.** (3 and 6 rue du Jour, 1er, tel. 45–08–
Casual 49–89) has knitwear separates that are wardrobe basics for young Parisians.

Inès de la Fressange (14 av. Montaigne, 8e, tel. 47–23–08–94), the former Chanel super-model, creates casual looks based on evergreen V-neck sweaters and slim, velvet jeans.

Sonia Rykiel (175 blvd. St-Germain, 6e, tel. 49–54–60–60 and 79 rue Fbg. St-Honoré, 8e, tel. 42–65–20–81) singlehandedly made cotton velour into a recognized fashion statement.

Suzette Idier (9 rue de Birague, 4e, tel. 42–77–72–52) runs an intimate, pocket-sized boutique chockful of superb "little black dresses," elegant daywear, and all the latest Paris accessories.

Clothing **Brummel** (Au Printemps department store, 64
(Men's) blvd. Haussmann, 9e, tel. 42–82–50–00) is Paris's menswear fashion leader: six floors of suits, sportswear, underwear, coats, ties, and accessories in all price ranges.

Charvet (28 pl. Vendôme, 1er, tel. 42–60–30–70) is the Parisian equivalent of a London tailor or New York's Brooks Brothers: a conservative, aristocratic institution famed for made-to-measure shirts and exquisite ties and accessories.

Dominique Morlotti (25 rue St-Sulpice, 6e, tel. 43–54–89–89) offers an easy-going approach to menswear. Moderately priced designer separates have that debonair Parisian flair.

Kenzo (3 pl. des Victoires, 2e, tel. 40–39–72–03, and 17 blvd. Raspail, 7e, tel. 45–49–33–75) brings exhuberant color and fantasy to his menswear collections. Move on if you're looking for a classic three-piece suit.

Clothing (Resale) **Réciproque** (95, 101, and 123 rue de la Pompe, 16e, tel. 47–04–30–28 [women's] and 47–27–93–52 [menswear]) is Paris's most exclusive swap shop. Savings are significant: 4,200 frs for a brocade Nina Ricci dinner suit, 300 frs for Camille Unglick shoes. Closed Mondays and from the end of July through August.

Fabrics **Rodin** (36 av. Champs-Elysées, 8e, tel. 43–59–58–82) and **Bouchara** (54 blvd. Haussmann, 9e, tel. 42–80–66–95) sell top-quality apparel and upholstery fabrics.

Food **Bread** **Poilâne** (8 rue du Cherche-Midi, 6e, tel. 45–48–42–59) produces the most famous bread in the world. The chewy sourdough loaves are sold in hundreds of Paris restaurants and shops and are airmailed to U.S. and Tokyo restaurants every day.

Candy and Chocolate **La Maison du Chocolat** (52 rue François 1er, 8e, tel. 47–23–38–25) is heaven for cocoa purists. Take home chocolates, ice cream, and other treats, or meet a friend in the tearoom for sinfully rich hot chocolate and chocolate-mousse *frappés* (cold drinks). Take-out only at 8 rue de la Madeleine, 9e, tel. 47–42–86–52 and 225 rue du Fbg. St-Honoré, 8e, tel. 42–27–39–44.

Gourmet Shops **Fauchon** (26–28–30 pl. de la Madeleine, 8e, tel. 47–42–60–11) and **Hédiard** (21 pl. de la Madeleine, 8e, tel. 42–66–44–36) sell prestigious house brands of pâté, mustard, honey, jellies, and private-label champagne, plus sumptuous produce from around the world.

Jewelry Most of the big names are based near the place Vendôme. Designer costume and semiprecious jewelry is sold in most of the av. Montaigne and rue du Faubourg St-Honoré boutiques.

Cartier (7 and 23 pl. Vendôme, 1er, tel. 42–61–55–55) has two less formal "Les Must" boutiques, which carry lighters, pens, watches, key-chains, and other gift items.

Lingerie **Chantal Thomass** (1 rue Vivienne, 1er, tel. 40–15–02–36) sets the right mood for her trademark black-lace hosiery, satin corsets, and feather-trimmed negligees in this plush, pink velvet boutique that resembles a Victorian bordello.

Natari (7 pl. Vendôme, 1er, tel. 42–96–22–94) seduces all, with selections for every pocketbook. Movie-star lingerie and peignoir sets come in pure silk or washable synthetic versions.

Music/Records **FNAC** (Forum des Halles, 1er, tel. 40–41–40–00; 26 av. Ternes, 17e, tel. 44–09–18–00; and 136 rue de Rennes, 6e, tel. 49–54–30–00) is a high-profile French chain selling music; photo, TV, and audio equipment; and books.

Virgin Megastore (52–60 av. des Champs-Elysées, 8e, tel. 40–74–06–48) has acres of CD's and tapes—everything from classic to rap—plus a book division.

Perfumes **Annick Goutal** (14 rue de Castiglione, 1er, tel. 42–60–52–82) is a gilt-and-ivory cream puff selling this exclusive signature perfume line.

Guerlain (68 av. des Champs Elysées, 8e, tel. 47–89–71–84, and 47 rue Bonaparte, 6e, tel. 43–26–71–19) boutiques are the only authorized Paris outlets for legendary perfumes like Shalimar, Jicky, Vol de Nuit, Mitsouko, and Chamade.

Scarves **Hermès** (24 rue du Fbg. St-Honoré, 8e, tel. 40–17–47–17) clocks a scarf sale every 20 seconds before the Christmas holidays! The all-silk *carrés*—truly fashion icons—are legendary for their brilliant colors and intricate designs, which change yearly.

Souleiado (78 rue de Seine, 6e, tel. 43–54–62–25, and 83 av. Paul Doumer, 16e, tel. 42–24–99–

34) uses traditional Provençal patterns for cotton scarves, quilted bags, and linens.

Shoes **Laurent Mercadel** (31 rue Tronchet, 8e, tel. 42–66–01–28, and 3 pl. des Victoires, 1er, tel. 45–08–84–44) offers classic styles updated with unusual accents.

Stéphane Kélian (23 blvd. de la Madeleine, 1er, tel. 42–96–01–84, and 6 pl. des Victoires, 2e, tel. 42–61–55–60) creates chic, high-style shoes that are also comfortable for men and women.

Tablewares **Au Bain Marie** (8 rue Boissy d'Anglas, 8e, tel. *China and* 42–66–59–74) is an enchanted kingdom for ama- *Crystal* teur and professional cooks. Come here for crockery, porcelain, and a world-class collection of cookbooks.

Lalique (11 rue Royale, 8e, tel. 42–66–52–40) crystal vases and statuettes are prized for their sinuous, romantic forms and delicate design.

Geneviève Lethu (28 rue St-Antoine, 4e, tel. 42–74–21–25) is a homey, casual shop selling tea services, potpourri mixtures, and table linens for your real or imagined country house.

Although there aren't any bargains at the **Baccarat Crystal showroom** (30 bis rue de Paradis, 10e, tel. 47–70–64–30), this elegant, red-carpeted spot with a fascinating in-house museum is well worth a visit.

Toys **Au Nain Bleu** (406–410 rue St-Honoré, 8e, tel. 42–60–39–01) is a high-price wonderland, with elaborate dollhouses, miniature sports cars, and enchanting hand-carved rocking horses.

Le Monde en Marche (34 rue Dauphine, 6e, tel. 43–26–66–53) specializes in unusual, old-fashioned wooden toys.

Shopping Arcades

The various shopping arcades, or *passages*, scattered around Paris often date back to the 19th century, and most have been splendidly restored. Their arching glass roofs, mosaic or marble flooring, and brass lamps are now set off to full advantage.

Most are conveniently located in the central 1st and 2nd arrondissements on the Right Bank. Our favorite is **Galerie Vivienne** (4 rue des Petits-Champs, 2e) between the Stock Exchange

(Bourse) and the Palais-Royal. **Galerie Véro-Dodat** (19 rue Jean-Jacques Rousseau, 1er) has painted ceilings and slender copper pillars. You'll find an arcade called **Passage des Pavillons** at 6 rue de Beaujolais, 1er, near the Palais-Royal gardens; and **Passage des Princes** at 97 rue de Richelieu, 2e. **Passage des Panoramas** (11 blvd. Montmartre, 2e) is the oldest of them all, opened in 1800.

Markets

Food Markets   Paris's open-air food markets are among the city's most colorful attractions. Every *quartier* (district) has one, although many are open only a few days each week. Sunday morning, till 1 PM, is usually a good time to go; Monday is the day these markets are likely to be closed.

Many of the better-known markets are located in areas you'd visit for sightseeing; our favorites are on **rue de Buci**, 6e (open daily); **rue Mouffetard,** 5e; and **rue Lepic** in Montmartre (the latter two best on weekends). The **Marché d'Aligre** (open Sat., Sun., and Mon. mornings) is a bit farther out, beyond the Bastille on rue d'Aligre in the 12th arrondissement, but you won't see many tourists in this less-affluent area of town, and Parisians from all over the city know it and love it. The prices come tumbling down as the morning draws to a close.

Flower and   Paris's main flower market is located right in the
Bird Markets   heart of the city on Ile de la Cité, between Notre Dame and the Palais de Justice. It's open every day except Sunday, when a bird market takes its place, and Monday, when it's closed.

Flea Markets   The **Marché aux Puces** on Paris's northern boundary (Métro: Porte de Clignancourt) still attracts the crowds, but its once unbeatable prices are now a feature of the past. This century-old labyrinth of alleyways packed with antiques dealers and junk stalls now spreads for over a square mile. *Open Sat., Sun., and Mon.*

4　Dining

We can wire money to every major city in Europe almost as fast as you can say, "Zut alors! J'ai perdu mes valises".

How fast? We can send money in 10 minutes or less, to 13,500 locations in over 68 countries worldwide. That's faster than any other international money transfer service. And when you're *sans* luggage, every minute counts.

MoneyGram from American Express® is available throughout Europe. For more information please contact your local American Express Travel Service Office or call: 44-71-839-7541 in England; 33-1-47777000 in France; or 49-69-21050 in Germany. In the United States call 1-800-MONEYGRAM.

MoneyGram
INTERNATIONAL MONEY TRANSFERS.

519 M.P.H.

190 M.P.H.

75 M.P.H.

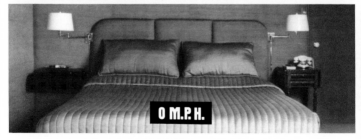

0 M.P.H.

WE LET YOU SEE EUROPE AT YOUR OWN PACE.

Regardless of your personal speed limits, Rail Europe offers everything to get you over, around and through anywhere you want in Europe. For more information, call your travel agent or **1-800-4-EURAIL**.

OFFICIAL DISTRIBUTOR
Rail Europe
OF THE EURAIL PASS

By Robert Noah

Robert Noah is the founder of Paris en Cuisine, *a company that offers food-related tours in Paris and elsewhere in France, and the editor of its English-language newsletter on French food.*

Whether your dream meal in Paris is savoring truffle-studded foie gras from Limoges china, or breaking the crust of a steaming cassoulet in a thick crockery bowl, you can find it here. For most visitors, the prospect of eating here is exciting; for many, it's the main reason for a trip. It's certainly possible to have a bad meal here. Yet the city's restaurants exist principally for the demanding Parisians themselves, for whom every meal is—if not a way of life—certainly an event worthy of their undivided attention.

Generally, Paris restaurants are open from noon to about 2, and from 7:30 or 8 to 10 or 10:30. Brasseries have longer hours and often serve all day and late into the evening; some are open 24 hours. The iconoclastic wine bars do as they want, frequently serving hot food only through lunch and cold assortments of *charcuterie* and cheese until a late afternoon or early evening close.

Because most restaurants are open for only a few set hours for lunch and dinner, and because meals are much longer affairs here than they are in the United States, we strongly advise you to make reservations. Most wine bars do not take reservations; reservations are also unnecessary for brasserie and café meals at odd hours. If you want nonsmoking, make this clear when you reserve. Though the law requires all restaurants to provide a nonsmoking area, this is sometimes limited to a very few tables.

All establishments must post their menus outside, so study them carefully before deciding to enter. Most restaurants offer two basic types of menu: à la carte and fixed price (*prix fixe*, or *un menu*). The prix-fixe menu will usually offer the best value, though choices are limited. Most menus begin with a first-course section, often subdivided into cold and hot starters, followed by fish and poultry, then meat; it's rare today that anyone orders something from all three. However, outside of brasseries, wine bars, and other simple places, it's inappropriate to order just one dish, as you'll understand when you see the waiter's expression.

All prices include tax and tip (*service compris* or *prix nets*). No additional tip is expected, though

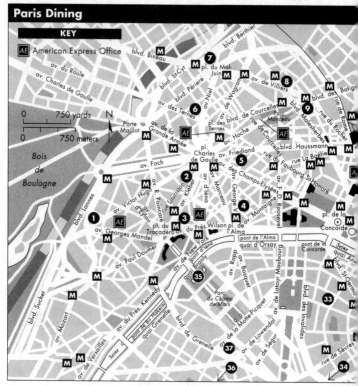

Paris Dining

KEY

AE American Express Office

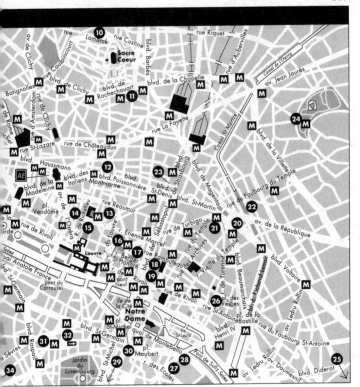

pocket change left on the table in simple places, or an additional 5% of the bill in better restaurants, is appreciated.

The following credit card abbreviations are used: AE, American Express; DC, Diners Club; MC, MasterCard; and V, Visa.

Highly recommended restaurants are indicated by a ★.

Category	Cost*
Very Expensive	over 550 frs
Expensive	300 frs–550 frs
Moderate	175 frs–300 frs
Inexpensive	under 175 frs

* *per person, including tax and service but not drinks*

1st Arrondissement (Louvre)

Very Expensive **Le Grand Véfour.** This sumptuously decorated restaurant is perhaps the prettiest in Paris, and its 18th-century origins make it one of the oldest. Chef Guy Martin impresses with his unique blend of sophisticated yet rustic dishes, including langoustines with calves' ear and cabbage ravioli with truffle cream. Luminaries from Napoléon to Colette have frequented this intimate address under the arcades of the Palais-Royal; you can request to be seated at their preferred table. *17 rue Beaujolais, Métro: Palais-Royal, tel. 42–96–56–27. Reservations 1 week in advance essential. Jacket and tie required. AE, DC, MC, V. Closed Sat. lunch, Sun., and Aug.*

Expensive **Pierre.** M. and Mme. Dez are always on hand to greet you in their long, two-dining-room address, a classic Parisian restaurant next to the Comédie Française. The many habitués return for the house specialties and want no contemporary gastronomic foolishness. Try the foie gras, pike *quenelles*, *beef à la ficelle*, and *tarte Tatin*. Dinner starts at 7 PM to accommodate Comédie Française theatergoers. *10 rue de Richelieu, Métro: Palais-Royal, tel. 42–96–09–17. Reser-*

vations advised. Dress: casual but elegant. DC,
MC, V. Closed Sat., Sun., and Aug.

Moderate **Le Petit Bourbon.** This charming restaurant of-
★ fers two fixed-price menus, one in the Inexpensive category. On both, first and main courses
such as mushroom terrine with shellfish sauce,
stuffed rabbit medallions, and chocolate soup
transcend the ordinary. The intimate dining
room has exposed stone walls, cream colors, and
pretty paintings of the Midi region. *15 rue du*
Roule, Métro: Louvre, tel. 40–26–08–93. Reser-
vations advised. Dress: casual. MC, V. Closed
Sun., Mon.

Pharamond. A Halles landmark since its found-
ing in 1870. No one would dare touch the poly-
chrome tiles and mosaics, mirrors, and
handsome woodwork, or the classic bistro menu
with Norman specialties such as scallops in ci-
der, grilled meats, *tripes à la mode de Caen*, and
souffléed potatoes. *24 rue de la Grande*
Truanderie, Métro: Les Halles, tel. 42–33–06–
72. Reservations advised. Dress: casual. AE,
DC, MC, V. Closed Sun., Mon. lunch, and mid-
July–mid-Aug.

2nd Arrondissement (Stock Exchange)

Moderate **Le Grand Colbert.** This very pretty brasserie,
owned by the Bibliothèque Nationale, is airy
and light, with its frosted glass and many mirrors. The large menu, which includes oysters,
herring fillets with potatoes, snails, and grilled
meats, has something for every taste. Waiters in
their black and whites with long aprons complete the picture of a classic brasserie. It's open
until 1 AM. *2 rue Vivienne, Métro: Bourse, tel.*
42–86–87–88. Reservations advised. Dress: ca-
sual. AE, DC, MC, V.

3rd Arrondissement (Le Marais/Beaubourg)

Inexpensive **Chez Jenny.** Order the filling choucroute Jenny
★ and a carafe of Alsatian wine, then sit back and
watch the bustle at this large Alsatian brasserie
decorated with museum-quality marquetry and
woodwork. Waitresses in regional costume
wend their way through many salons on two lev-
els, serving forth hearty fare. Though the clien-

tele is not the chic crowd of some other brasseries, everyone's having just as much fun. *39 blvd. du Temple, Métro: République, tel. 42–74–75–75. Reservations advised. Dress: casual. AE, DC, MC, V.*

4th Arrondissement (Le Marais/Ile St-Louis)

Expensive   **Benoît.** Founded in 1912, Benoît retains the feel
★   of a classic bistro—with its frosted glass, lace curtains, polished brass, and a warm welcome—despite its high prices. Try the layered beef tongue–foie gras Lucullus, marinated salmon, cassoulet, or game in season. Patrons debate the merits of the front or back room, but conviviality reigns in both. *20 rue St. Martin, Métro: Châtelet, tel. 42–72–25–76. Reservations required. Dress: casual. No credit cards. Closed Sat., Sun., Aug.*

Moderate   **Le Grizzli.** It's said this turn-of-the-century bistro was one of the last to have dancing bears as entertainment—thus the name. Today's owner gets many of his ingredients—especially the wonderful ham and cheeses—from his native Auvergne. Several dishes are cooked on hot slate, including salmon and lamb. There's an interesting selection of wines from Southwest France. Prices here are at the low end of our Moderate range. *7 rue St. Martin, Métro: Châtelet, tel. 48–87–77–56. Reservations advised. Dress: casual. MC, V. Closed Sun., Mon. lunch.*

Inexpensive   **Baracane.** This is one of the best values in the
★   Marais district. The owner oversees the menu, full of the robust specialties of his native Southwest France, including rabbit confit, braised oxtail with foie gras, and pear poached in wine and cassis. A reasonable dinner menu and cheaper menu at lunch keep the Baracane solidly in the Inexpensive range. *38 rue des Tournelles, Métro: Bastille, tel. 42–71–43–33. Reservations advised. Dress: casual. MC, V. Closed Sat. lunch, Sun.*

5th Arrondissement (Latin Quarter)

Very Expensive ★ **La Tour d'Argent.** Dining at this temple to haute cuisine is a theatrical and unique event—from apéritifs in the ground-floor bar to dinner in the top-floor dining room, with its breath-taking view of Notre Dame. In recent years elegant owner Claude Terrail has hired a series of young chefs, and today's menu is a mix of Tour classics and contemporary creations. Venerable favorites such as *caneton* Tour d'Argent (pressed duck), quenelles André Terrail, and filets de sole Cardinal have been lightened, and new dishes added, including scallop salad with truffles and double-thick lamb chops with carrots. The wine list is one of the greatest in the world. *15 quai de la Tournelle, Métro: Cardinal Lemoine, tel. 43-54-23-31. Reservations required at least one week in advance. Jacket and tie required at dinner, advised at lunch. AE, DC, MC, V. Closed Mon.*

Moderate **Campagne et Provence.** This small establishment on the quai across from Notre Dame offers fresh, colorful, Provençal-inspired cuisine including vegetables stuffed with cod brandade and ratatouille omelettes. The list of reasonably priced regional wines helps keep prices down—almost in the Inexpensive range. *25 quai de la Tournelle, Métro: Maubert-Mutualité, tel. 43-54-05-17. Reservations advised. Dress: casual. MC, V. Closed Sat. lunch, Sun.*

6th Arrondissement (Luxembourg)

Moderate **La Rôtisserie d'En Face.** A long rotisserie is part of the attractive country-elegant decor at this bistro created by renowned chef Jacques Cagna. The cuisine includes roast chicken with mashed potatoes, grilled salmon with spinach, and chocolate éclairs. The menu is fixed-price only, and it's cheaper at lunch. Dinner is two set seatings only. *2 rue Christine, Métro: Odéon, tel. 43-26-40-98. MC, V. Closed Sat. lunch, Sun.*

Inexpensive **Aux Charpentiers.** This old, large neighborhood bistro in St-Germain-des-Prés is eternally popular with students, locals, and tourists. Enjoy the homemade preparations of foie gras, cod *aïoli* (garlic mayonnaise) with vegetables, boeuf à la mode, and chocolate mousse—and the boisterous atmosphere. *10 rue Mabillon, Métro: Mabillon, tel. 43-26-30-05. Reservations advised. Dress: casual. AE, DC, MC, V. Closed Sun.*

7th Arrondissment (Invalides)

Very Expensive
★

L'Arpège. This small, striking restaurant one block from the Rodin Museum is currently one of the most talked-about of Paris's restaurants. It features the cuisine of young chef-owner Alain Passard, whose menu is both original (lobster/turnip starter in a sweet-sour vinaigrette, stuffed sweet tomato) and classic (beef Burgundy, pressed duck). With its curving, hand-crafted wood panels and wrought-iron window frames, the decor is unusually minimalist. Service, although young and energetic, sometimes falls behind. *84 rue de Varenne, Métro: Varenne, tel. 45-51-47-33. Reservations advised. Dress: casual but elegant. AE, DC, MC, V. Closed Sat., Sun. lunch, Aug.*

Jules Verne. Distinctive all-black decor, stylish service, and a top chef—not to mention a location at 400 feet, on the second level of the Eiffel Tower—have made the Jules Verne one of the hardest dinner reservations to get in Paris. Asparagus and foie gras aspic, sole fillet with crab sauce, and veal medallions with bell pepper sauce are examples of Chef Bariteau's colorful, flavorful cuisine. The restaurant is open daily, and a lunch table is easier to snag. *Eiffel Tower, Métro: Bir-Hakeim, tel. 45-55-61-44. Reservations 2 months in advance for dinner at window table. Jacket and tie required. AE, DC, MC, V.*

Inexpensive
★

Au Sauvignon. A young, modish, intellectual crowd fills this tiny wine bar, where you'll find the usual limited menu of *tartines*, or open-faced sandwiches, on the famous Poilâne loaf, topped with good-quality charcuterie, cheese, or both. The colorful murals will amuse you, but it's even more fun to people-watch from one of the tables set on the narrow sidewalk. *80 rue des Saints Pères, Métro: Sèvres-Babylone, tel. 45-48-04-69. No reservations. Dress: casual. No credit* cards. *Closed Sat. eve., Sun., Aug., Christmas week, and Easter.*

8th Arrondissement (Champs-Elysées)

Very Expensive ★ **Taillevent.** Many say it's the best restaurant in Paris. Within the wood-paneled main dining rooms of this mid-19th-century mansion you will find exceptional service that is never over-bearing, a stellar wine list, and the tempered classic cuisine of young chef Philippe Legendre. Among his signature dishes are celery turnover with morels and truffles and lamb with cabbage. Pastry chef Gilles Bajolle is one of the finest in Paris. Try his *nougatine glacée aux poires* (thin layers of nougatine and pear sherbet) or tarte Tatin with quince. Book months ahead. *15 rue Lamennais, Métro: Charles de Gaulle/Etoile, tel. 45-63-39-94. Reservations essential. Jacket and tie required. MC, V. Closed weekends, Aug.*

Moderate ★ **La Fermette Marbeuf.** It's a favorite haunt of French TV and movie stars, who like the spectacular Belle Epoque mosaics, tiles, and stained glass (discovered by accident when the restaurant was being redecorated), and appreciate the solid, updated classic cuisine. Try *gâteau* of chicken livers and sweetbreads, lamb navarin with vegetables, and bitter chocolate fondant. Prices here are exceptional, considering the quality of the food, the surroundings, and the neighborhood. The Fermette becomes animated late, around 9. *5 rue Marbeuf, Métro: Franklin Roosevelt, tel. 47-20-63-53. Reservations advised. Dress: casual but elegant. AE, DC, MC, V.*

Inexpensive **Berry's.** This tiny annex next door to the more expensive Le Grenadin, near the Parc Monceau, is a bargain. Talented chef-owner Patrick Cirotte prepares dishes of his native Berry region (veal simmered in red wine) and serves local wines, including fine Sancerres. Decor is lean and modern, the atmosphere young and upbeat. It's open until 1 AM. *46 rue de Naples, Métro: Villiers, tel. 40-75-01-56. Reservations advised. Dress: casual. AE, MC, V. Closed Sun.*

9th Arrondissement (Opéra)

Expensive **La Table d'Anvers.** One of the best restaurants
★ near Montmartre, it serves an interesting
menu, with Italian and Provençal touches in
dishes like gnocchi of langoustines and *girolles*
(wild mushrooms), saddle of rabbit with polen-
ta, and *croustillant* of asparagus with crab. The
Table's desserts, such as strawberry tart with
rhubarb, are among the best in Paris; serious
sweet-tooths can indulge in an all-dessert menu,
which includes a single token fish dish. *2 pl.
d'Anvers, Métro: Anvers, tel. 48–78–35–21.
Reservations advised. Dress: casual but elegant. AE, MC, V. Closed Sat. lunch, Sun., mid-
Aug.*

Inexpensive **Chartier.** This cavernous turn-of-the-century
restaurant enjoys a huge following among the
budget-minded, including students, solitary
bachelors, and tourists. You may find yourself
sharing a table with strangers as you study the
long, old-fashioned menu of such favorites as
hard-boiled eggs with mayonnaise, pâté, and
roast veal with spinach. *7 rue du Faubourg-
Montmartre, Métro: rue Montmartre, tel. 47–
70–86–29. No reservations. Dress: casual. No
credit cards.*

10th Arrondissement (République)

Moderate **Brasserie Flo.** This, the first of brasserie king
Jean-Paul Bucher's seven Paris addresses, is
hard to find down its passageway near the Gare
de l'Est, but worth the effort. The rich wood-
and stained-glass interior is typically Alsatian,
the service enthusiastic, and the brasserie standards such as shellfish, steak tartare, and
choucroute tasty. Order one of the carafes of Alsatian wine. It's open until 1:30 AM, with a special night-owl menu from 11 PM. *7 cour des
Petites Ecuries, Métro: Château d'Eau, tel. 47–
70–13–59. Reservations advised. Dress: casual
but elegant. AE, DC, MC, V. Closed Christmas
eve.*

11th Arrondissement (Bastille)

Moderate **Chez Philippe/Pyrénées-Cévennes.** Old-timers
★ still refer to this comfortable bistro by its origi-

nal name—Pyrénées-Cévennes—while others know it as Chez Philippe. The eclectic menu combines the cooking of Burgundy, central France—even Spain—in such dishes as snails in garlic butter, cassoulet, and paella. An attentive staff bustles amid cozy surroundings, with beamed ceiling and polished copper. *106 rue de la Folie-Méricourt, Métro: République, tel. 43-57-33-78. Reservations advised. Dress casual. MC, V. Closed weekends, Aug.*

Inexpensive **Astier.** You'll find remarkable value at this pleasant restaurant, where the prix-fixe menu (there's no à la carte) includes first and main courses, cheese (excellent), and dessert. Among high-quality dishes, try mussel soup with saffron, fricassée of beef cheeks, and plum clafoutis. Service can be rushed, but the enthusiastic crowd does not seem to mind. Study the excellent wine list, which has some surprising buys. *44 rue Jean-Pierre Timbaud, Métro: République, tel. 43-57-16-35. Reservations advised. Dress: casual. MC, V. Closed weekends, Aug.*

12th Arrondissement (Gare de Lyon)

Expensive **Au Trou Gascon.** The success of this Belle
★ Epoque establishment off the place Daumesnil enabled owner Alain Dutournier to open the now-renowned Carré des Feuillants in the 1st arrondissement. He's still the owner here, too, and continues to serve his personal version of the cuisine of Gascony, a region of outstanding ham, foie gras, lamb, and poultry. His white chocolate mousse is now a classic. *40 rue Taine, Métro: Daumesnil, tel. 43-44-34-26. Reservations advised. Dress: casual. AE, DC, MC, V. Closed weekends, Christmas week, Aug.*

14th Arrondissement (Montparnasse)

Expensive **La Cagouille.** This is one of the best fish restau-
★ rants in Paris. Bear-like Gérard Allemandou moved his intimate and very successful *bistro à poissons* to this vast, modern space on the somewhat sterile place Brancusi several years ago. But his style remains the same: Few sauces or adornments mask the fresh, clean flavors of fish, from elegant sole and turbot to more pedestrian

sardines and mackeral. Besides his excellent wine list, La Cagouille has the finest collection of Cognacs in the city. There's a large terrace for warm-weather dining. *10–12 pl. Brancusi, Métro: Gaité, tel. 43–22–09–01. Reservations advised. Dress: casual but elegant. AE, MC, V.*

Moderate **Le Pavillon Montsouris.** This bucolic building on
★ the edge of Parc Montsouris was recently restored, and the pretty pastel interior and large terrace facing the park make for a charming spot on a sunny day. A multichoice, prix-fixe menu is a real bargain, and dishes prepared by the bright, young chef here are fresh and interesting. Try mussel soup with langoustines, *hachis Parmentier* (a kind of rich man's shepherd's pie) with foie gras and duck, and mango clafoutis. Service can slow down during peak times; go when you have time for a leisurely meal. *20 rue Gazan, Métro: RER Cité-Universitaire, tel. 45–88–38–52. Reservations advised. Dress: casual. DC, MC, V.*

15th Arrondissement (Front de Seine)

Expensive **Morot-Gaudry.** Located on top of a building near
★ the Ecole Militaire, this popular address offers the luxury of well-spaced tables and an unusual outlook over Paris. Chef-owner Jean-Pierre Morot-Gaudry prepares a personalized cuisine that's a combination of classic and modern. Recommended are scallops with Jerusalem artichokes, veal blanquette, and chocolate millefeuille with wild raspberries. The menu marries a different wine with each dish; the prix-fixe menu at lunch puts Morot-Gaudry in our Moderate range. *6 rue de la Cavalerie, Métro: Motte-Picquet, tel. 47–34–62–92. Reservations advised. Dress: casual. AE, MC, V. Closed weekends.*

Moderate **Le Clos Morillons.** The chef here has made many trips to the Far East, and his cuisine incorporates such oriental flavorings as sesame and ginger. But the menu is unmistakably French, with its delicious terrine of potato with foie gras, roast guinea fowl, and the all-chocolate dessert (several kinds of chocolate desserts on one plate). Added pluses are the professional service in the quiet dining room, an interesting wine list emphasizing Loire wines, and fixed-price menus at lunch and dinner that put the Clos in the low-Moderate and Inexpensive ranges. *50 rue Morillons, Métro: Convention, tel. 48–28–04–37. Reservations advised. Dress: casual. MC, V. Closed Sat. lunch, Sun.*

16th Arrondissement (Trocadéro/Bois de Boulogne)

Very Expensive ★ **Jamin/Robuchon.** Surely it's the hardest reservation to obtain in France. Chef-owner Joël Robuchon, though under 50, has already attained cult status, and his influence on cooks around the globe is great. Under his inspired vision, everything from John Dory with ginger and cream of cauliflower with caviar to saddle of lamb in a salt crust and even pig's head become visual and gustatory revelations. Antoine Hernandez, chef-sommelier, is a gentle guide through the impressive wine list, and service in general is attentive and professional. The pretty, pastel dining room is less impressive than the cuisine; the restaurant is due to move into its own *hôtel particulier* in the future. *32 rue de Longchamp, Métro: Trocadéro, tel. 47–27–12–27. Reservations essential. Jacket and tie advised. MC, V. Closed weekends, July.*

★ **Le Vivarois.** Chef-owner Claude Peyrot is one of the most inspired and creative of contemporary French chefs, though his cooking can be uneven. He is a master with fish and puff pastry, his *bavarois* of red bell pepper (a creamy, molded concoction) is oft-imitated, and his original dishes shine: scallops with sesame and ginger, *rissolette* of lamb's feet with artichokes and basil, and chocolate soufflé with chicory ice cream. Service is not always up to par. *192 av. Victor Hugo, Métro: Rue de la Pompe, tel. 47–04–04–31. Reservations advised. Dress: casual. AE, DC, MC, V. Closed weekends, Aug.*

Moderate **Bistrot de l'Etoile Lauriston.** This attractive, subdued establishment features the intelligent yet homey cuisine of Chef William Ledeuil. His full-flavored dishes include stuffed, gratinéed zucchini, ravioli with *pistou*, and lamb sautéed with rosemary. An upscale crowd includes many Americans. *19 rue Lauriston, Métro: Charles* *de Gaulle, tel. 40–67–11–16. Reservations advised. Dress: casual. AE, MC, V. Closed Sun.*

17th Arrondissement (Monceau/Clichy)

Very Expensive **Apicius.** Chef-owner Jean-Pierre Vigato excels at mixing the humble with the rarified, as he does here in dishes from duck *tourte* (pie) and pig's foot to roasted sweetbreads and Bresse chicken cooked in salt. A good-looking crowd occupies the airy, flower-filled dining rooms. *122 av. de Villiers, Métro: Pereire, tel. 43–80–19–66. Reservations advised. Dress: casual but elegant. AE, MC, V. Closed weekends and Aug.*

Expensive **Augusta.** In this fine fish restaurant in a prosperous corner of the 17th, the menu combines fish classics with chef Lionel Maître's original creations. Sample mussels with garlic butter, bouillabaisse with potatoes, or langoustines with vanilla. At least one meat dish is always offered. The comfortable dining room invites lingering. *98 rue de Toqueville, Métro: Malesherbes, tel. 47–63–39–97. Reservations advised. Dress: casual but elegant. MC, V. Closed Sat. lunch, Sun., Aug.*

Moderate **La Niçoise.** Posters of Nice adorn the simple upstairs dining room, and Mediterranean flavors emerge from the kitchen at this enjoyable Niçoise oasis. Try ricotta ravioli with basil, or *petits farcis Niçois* (stuffed vegetables). Moderately priced Provençal wines help keep prices down. *4 rue Pierre Demours, Métro: Ternes, tel. 45–74–42–41. Reservations advised. Dress: casual. AE, DC, MC, V. Closed Sat. lunch, Sun.*

18th Arrondissement (Montmartre)

Very Expensive **A. Beauvilliers.** Pickwickian owner Edouard Carlier is a born party-giver, and his flower-filled restaurant is one of the most festive in Paris. The three dining rooms are filled with his personal collection of paintings and valuable *bibelots*, and a tiny, vine-covered terrace makes for delightful summer dining. Chefs here come and go, but Mr. Carlier maintains quality, serving both original creations and reinterpreted classics. Recommended are the red mullet *en escabèche* (in a peppery marinade) and foie gras, lobster, and sweetbread *tourte*. The mouth-

puckering lemon tart is not to be missed. One
drawback: Service can be distant if you are not
known. *52 rue Lamarck, Métro: Lamarck-
Caulaincourt, tel. 42–54–54–42. Reservations
essential. Jacket and tie advised. AE, MC, V.
Closed Sun., Mon. lunch, and Sept.*

19th Arrondissement (La Villette)

Expensive **Le Pavillon Puebla.** This turn-of-the-century
building in the spectacular Parc des Buttes-
Chaumont is a bit hard to find, but feels wonder-
fully removed from the bustle of the city. Chef
Vergès prepares an original, flavorful cuisine,
including oyster ravioli with curry, lamb
tournedos with truffle juice, and *gâteau* of
crêpes and apples. Mme. Vergès oversees the
elegant dining rooms and large terrace. *Parc
Buttes-Chaumont (entrance rue Botzaris),
Métro: Buttes-Chaumont, tel. 42–08–92–62.
Reservations advised. Dress: casual but elegant. MC, V. Closed Sun., Mon., mid-Aug.*

5 Lodging

American Express offers Travelers Cheques built for two.

American Express® Cheques *for Two*. The first Travelers Cheques that allow either of you to use them because both of you have signed them. And only one of you needs to be present to purchase them.

Cheques *for Two* are accepted anywhere regular American Express Travelers Cheques are, which is just about everywhere. So stop by your bank, AAA* or any American Express Travel Service Office and ask for Cheques *for Two*.

Updated by
David Downie

Our criteria when selecting the hotels reviewed below were quality, location, and—where possible—character. Generally, there are more Right Bank hotels offering luxury—or at any rate formality—than there are on the Left Bank, where hotels tend to be smaller but often loaded with character. Despite the huge choice of hotels here, you should always reserve well in advance, especially if you're determined to stay in a specific hotel. You can do this by telephoning ahead, then writing or faxing for confirmation. If you are asked to send a deposit, make sure you discuss refund policies before mailing your check or money order. Always ask for some form of written confirmation of your reservation, detailing the duration of your stay, the price, location and type of your room (single or double, twin beds or double), and bathroom (*see below*).

Many Paris hotels have idiosyncrasies—some charming, others less so. Rooms are not always perfectly square, floors not always perfectly flat. The standard French double bed is slightly smaller than its American counterpart. Airconditioning is uncommon in all but the most luxurious hotels. The most enduring example of quirkiness is French plumbing, which sometimes looks like avant-garde sculpture. Shared toilets or bathrooms down the hall, though increasingly rare, are still found in many modest establishments. Our reviews indicate the number of rooms with full bath facilities including tub (*baignoire*) or shower (*douche*), and number of rooms with shared baths. Make sure you know what you are getting when you book.

Almost all Paris hotels charge extra for breakfast, with prices ranging from 30 francs to over 100 francs per person in luxury establishments. Hotels generally assume you will be having breakfast there, and will add the breakfast charge to your bill automatically. If you don't want to have breakfast at the hotel, say so when you check in. For anything more than the standard Continental breakfast of *café au lait* (coffee with hot milk) and *baguette* (bread) or croissants, the price will be higher.

You'll notice that the French government grades hotels from four-star deluxe to one star, and that the stars appear on a shield on the hotel's facade. Theoretically, the ratings depend on amenities and price. They can be misleading, however, since many hotels prefer to be understarred for tax reasons. Many two- and three-star establishments offer excellent price-to-quality ratios. We list hotels by price, but often a hotel in a certain price category will have a few rooms that are less expensive; it's worthwhile to ask. Rates must be posted in all rooms, and all extra charges clearly shown.

Unless otherwise stated, the hotels reviewed below have elevators, and rooms have TVs and telephones. Additional facilities, such as restaurants and health clubs, are listed at the end of each review.

The following credit card abbreviations are used: AE, American Express; DC, Diners Club; MC, MasterCard; and V, Visa.

Highly recommended lodgings are indicated by a star ★.

Category	Cost*
Very Expensive	over 1,200 frs
Expensive	750 frs–1,200 frs
Moderate	450 frs–750 frs
Inexpensive	under 450 frs

All prices are for a standard double room, including tax and service.

1st Arrondissement (Louvre)

Very Expensive ★ **Inter-Continental.** An aura of elegant luxury reigns throughout this exquisite late-19th-century hotel, one of the largest of the city's top hotels. It was designed by the architect of the Paris Opéra, Garnier. Three of its gilt and stuccoed public rooms are official historic monuments. Spacious guest rooms overlook quiet inner courtyards. In summer, breakfast on the patio is a delicious experience. Service is impeccable. *3 rue de Castiglione, 75001, Métro:*

Concorde, tel. 44–77–11–11, fax 44–77–14–60. 380 rooms with bath, 70 suites with bath. English spoken. Facilities: 2 restaurants, bar, patio. AE, DC, MC, V.

Expensive **Régina.** Set in the handsome place des
★ Pyramides, this Art Nouveau gem stuffed with fine antiques is pleasantly old-fashioned. Request a room overlooking the Louvre and the Tuileries Gardens. 2 pl. des Pyramides, 75001, Métro: Tuileries, tel. 42–60–31–10, fax 40–15–95–16. 120 rooms and 10 suites, all with bath. English spoken. Facilities: restaurant (closed August), bar. AE, DC, MC, V.

Moderate **Britannique.** A friendly, family-owned hotel in a restored 19th-century building, the Britannique has a handsome winding staircase and nicely decorated, soundproofed rooms. Ask for a room on one of the top three floors. 20 av. Victoria, 75001, Métro: Châtelet, tel. 42–33–74–59, fax 42–33–82–65. 25 rooms with bath, 15 with shower. English spoken. AE, DC, V.

Inexpensive **Lille.** You won't find a less expensive base for exploring the Louvre than this hotel, located a short distance from the Cour Carrée. The facade got a face-lift a few years ago, but the somewhat shabby interior and minimal plumbing down long corridors was not upgraded. Hence the rock-bottom prices. Still, the Lille is a slice of Old Paris. There's no elevator, and not all rooms have TVs or phones. 8 rue du Pélican, 75001, Métro: Palais-Royal, tel. 42–33–33–42. 5 rooms with shower, 8 with shared bath. Some English spoken. No credit cards.

2nd Arrondissement (Stock Exchange)

Expensive **Gaillon-Opéra.** The oak beams, stone walls, and
★ marble tiles of the Gaillon-Opéra single it out as one of the most charming hotels in the Opéra neighborhood. The plants throughout and a flower-filled patio also delight. There's a small bar but no restaurant. 9 rue Gaillon, 75002, Métro: Opéra, tel. 47–42–47–74, fax 47–42–01–23. 26 rooms and 1 suite, all with bath. English spoken. Facilities: bar. AE, DC, MC, V.

Moderate **Choiseul-Opéra.** The historic, classical facade of the Choiseul-Opéra, located between the Opéra

Paris Lodging

KEY

AE American Express Office

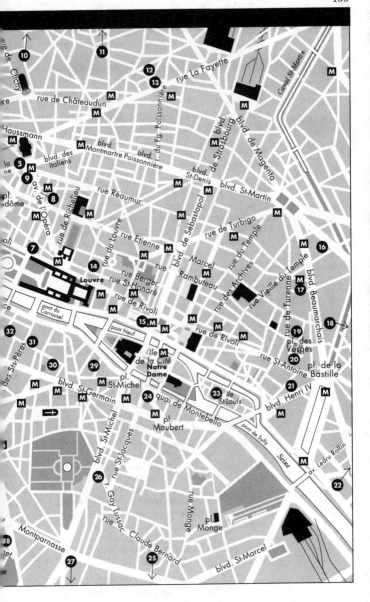

and place Vendôme, belies the strictly functional interior. The entrance hall, salon, and bar were remodeled in 1992, and many rooms were freshened up. Service is relaxed but efficient, and the staff are happy to try out their English on guests. There's no restaurant or bar. *1 rue Daunou, 75002, Métro: Opéra, tel. 42–61–70–41, fax 42–86–91–96. 30 rooms with bath, 15 with shower, 2 suites with bath. English spoken. AE, DC, MC, V.*

3rd Arrondissement (Le Marais/Beaubourg)

Very Expensive ★ **Pavillon de la Reine.** The best hotel in the Marais, it's set around two flower-filled courtyards behind the historic Queen's Pavilion on the 17th-century place des Vosges. Although this cozy mansion looks old, it was actually reconstructed from scratch in 1986 following original plans and using period timbers, rough-hewn paving stones, Louis XIII fireplaces, and antiques. Ask for a duplex with French windows overlooking the first courtyard (there are no rooms overlooking the place des Vosges). Breakfast is served in a vaulted cellar. *28 pl. des Vosges, 75003, Métro: Chemin Vert, tel. 42–77–96–40, fax 42–77–63–06. 31 rooms with bath, 24 suites with bath. English spoken. Facilities: cellar dining room, parking. AE, DC, MC, V.*

Moderate **Hôtel du Marais.** On the edge of the Marais, this small hotel in a restored old building is near the Bastille Opéra and the Picasso Museum. For extremely reasonable (borderline inexpensive) rates you get amenities generally reserved for more expensive hotels, such as minibars and color TVs in rooms. Some rooms have exposed beams; all are functional, soundproofed, and clean. *2 bis rue des Commines, 75003, Métro: Filles-du-Calvaire, tel. 48–87–78–27, fax 48–87–09–01. 12 rooms with bath, 27 with shower. Some English spoken. Facilities: minibar in rooms. AE, DC, MC, V.*

4th Arrondissement (Le Marais/Ile St-Louis)

Expensive ★ **Deux-Iles.** This converted 17th-century mansion on the Ile St-Louis has long won plaudits for charm and comfort. Flowers and plants are scattered around the stunning hall. The fabric-hung rooms, though small, have exposed beams and are fresh and airy. Ask for a room overlooking the little garden courtyard. There's no restaurant, but drinks are served in the cellar bar until 1 AM. The lounge is dominated by a fine chimneypiece and doubles as a second bar. *59 rue St-Louis-en-l'Ile, 75004, Métro: Pont-Marie, tel. 43–26–13–35, fax 43–29–60–25. 8 rooms with bath, 9 with shower. English spoken. Facilities: bar (closed Sun.). No credit cards.*

Moderate **Place des Vosges.** A loyal American clientele
★ swears by this small, historic hotel located on a charming street just off the exquisite square of the same name. Oak-beamed ceilings and rough-hewn stone in public areas and some of the guest rooms add to the atmosphere. Ask for the top-floor room, the hotel's largest, with a view of Marais rooftops. Some rooms, the size of walk-in closets, are inexpensive. There's a welcoming little breakfast room. *12 rue de Birague, 75004, Métro: Bastille, tel. 42–72–60–46, fax 42–72–02–64. 5 rooms with bath, 11 with shower. English spoken. AE, DC, V.*

Inexpensive **Castex.** This family-run, two-star hotel in a
★ 19th-century building is a real find. It was remodeled from top to bottom in 1989, and rooms are squeaky clean. The decor is strictly functional, but the extremely friendly owners and rock-bottom prices mean the Castex is often fully booked months ahead. There's a large American clientele. The eight least expensive rooms, two per floor, share toilets on the immaculate, well-lit landings. There's no elevator, and TV is in the lobby only. *5 rue Castex, 75004, Métro: Bastille, tel. 42–72–31–52, fax 42–72–57–91. 4 rooms with bath, 23 with shower. English spoken. MC, V.*

5th Arrondissement (Latin Quarter)

Expensive **Elysa Luxembourg.** The Elysa is what the
★ French call an *hôtel de charme.* Though the building is not large, most rooms are surprisingly spacious, and all are exquisitely maintained and refurbished yearly. Cream-colored furniture is set against pale blue or pink fabrics.

You'll find a minibar in every room and a breakfast lounge serving Continental or buffet breakfasts. The Elysa is one of the rare hotels in the city with a sauna. Rooms with shower are moderately priced. *6 rue Gay Lussac, 75005, Métro: Luxembourg, tel. 43–25–31–74, fax 46–34–56–27. 25 rooms with bath, 5 with shower. English spoken. Facilities: sauna. AE, DC, MC, V.*

Moderate **Esméralda.** Lovers of small, charming Parisian
★ hotels will want to stay at this simple lodging, where the rooms are a little dusty but positively exude timeworn Gallic charm. Esméralda is set in a fine 17th-century building opposite Notre Dame (request a room with a view), near Square Viviani. All the rooms are small—some are midget-size. Many have copies of 17th-century furniture. Those with showers on the landing are inexpensive. *4 rue St-Julien-le-Pauvre, 75005, Métro: St-Michel, tel. 43–54–19–20, fax 40–51–00–68. 16 rooms with bath, 3 with shower on the landing. Some English spoken. No credit cards.*

6th Arrondissement (Luxembourg)

Very **Relais Christine.** The Relais Christine is one of
Expensive the most appealing of the Left Bank hotels, im-
★ peccably luxurious yet oozing charm. The hotel is located on a quiet street between the Seine and the boulevard St-Germain and occupies some precious 16th-century cloisters. The best rooms look out over the central lawn. All are spacious and comfortable, particularly the duplexes on the upper floors. Air-conditioning and double-glazed windows add to their appeal. There's no restaurant, and only guests may use the bar. *3 rue Christine, 75006, Métro: St-Michel, tel. 43–26–71–80, fax 43–26–89–38. 34 rooms and 17 suites, all with bath. English spoken. Facilities: parking, bar. AE, DC, MC, V.*

Expensive **Hôtel d'Angleterre.** Some claim the Hôtel
★ d'Angleterre is the ultimate Left Bank hotel—a little small and shabby, but elegant and perfectly managed. The 18th-century building was originally the British ambassador's residence; later, Hemingway made it his Paris home. Room sizes and rates vary greatly, though all rooms are individually decorated. Some are imposing-

ly formal, others are homey and plain. Ask for one overlooking the courtyard. *44 rue Jacob, 75006, Métro: St-Germain-des-Prés, tel. 42–60–34–72, fax 42–60–16–93. 26 rooms and 3 suites, all with bath. English spoken. Facilities: bar, patio. AE, DC, MC, V.*

Moderate **Marronniers.** There are few better places in Par-
★ is than the Marronniers for great value and at-
mosphere. Located on appealing rue Jacob, the hotel is reached through a small courtyard. All rooms are light and full of character. Those on the attic floor have sloping ceilings, uneven floors, and terrific views over the church of St-Germain-des-Prés. The vaulted cellars have been converted into two atmospheric lounges. Prices can creep into the expensive range. *21 rue Jacob, 75006, Métro: St-Germain-des-Prés, tel. 43–25–30–60, fax 40–46–83–56. 17 rooms with bath, 20 with shower. English spoken. Facilities: bar. No credit cards.*

7th Arrondissement (Invalides)

Expensive **Université.** This appealingly converted 17th-
★ century town house is located between boule-
vard St-Germain and the Seine. Rooms have their original fireplaces and are decorated with English and French antiques. Ask for one of the two rooms with a terrace on the sixth floor. Though there's no restaurant, you can rent the vaulted cellar for parties. Drinks and snacks are served all day in the bar or, in good weather, in the courtyard. Rooms with shower are moderately priced. *22 rue de l'Université, 75007, Métro: Bac, tel. 42–61–09–39, fax 42–60–40–84. 20 rooms with bath, 7 with shower. English spoken. Facilities: bar. No credit cards.*

Moderate **Pavillon.** The entrance to the family-run Pavil-
★ lon lies behind a garden at the end of an alley off
rue St-Dominique, guaranteeing peace and quiet. Although some rooms in this former 19th-century convent are tiny, all have been redeco-
rated and feature Laura Ashley wallpaper and old prints. Breakfast is served in the little courtyard in summer. There's no elevator, but the hotel is only two stories high. *54 rue St-Dominique, 75007, Métro: Invalides, tel. 45–*

51–42–87, fax 45–51–32–79. 3 rooms with bath, 15 with shower. English spoken. AE, MC, V.

Inexpensive **Champ de Mars.** This simple, clean two-star hotel has one-star prices. Don't expect luxury or atmosphere, just a very good deal, in a nice neighborhood near the Eiffel Tower and Invalides. *7 rue Champ de Mars, 75007, Métro: Ecole Militaire, tel. 45–51–52–30. 19 rooms with bath, 6 with shower. Some English spoken. MC, V. Closed two weeks in mid-Aug.*

8th Arrondissement (Champs-Elysées)

Very Expensive ★ **Crillon.** In a city filled with world-class hotels, only the Crillon can provide a front-row seat to history, set as it is in two 18th-century town houses on the place de la Concorde, site of the French Revolution's infamous guillotine. Marie Antoinette, who met her end there, took singing lessons at the Hôtel de Crillon, where one of the original *grand appartments,* now sumptuous salons protected by the French National Historic Landmark Commission, has been named for the queen. Guests must pay dearly for a balcony overlooking the great square, with seemingly all of Paris at their feet; only the suites have them. Lesser mortals still get magnificent digs, individually decorated with Rococo and Directoire antiques, crystal and gilt wall sconces, and gold fittings. Most double rooms have separate sitting rooms, and the bathrooms, stocked with wonderful Annick Goutal toiletries, are clad in marble. The sheer quantity of the marble downstairs—in the lobby, the adjacent lounge, and especially the grand, top-rated Les Ambassadeurs restaurant is staggering. The staff anticipates your every need. *10 pl. de la Concorde, 75008, Métro: Concorde, tel. 44–71–15–00, fax 44–71–15–02. 120 rooms and 43 suites, all with bath. English spoken. Facilities: 2 restaurants, 2 bars, shop. AE, DC, MC, V.*

Expensive **Bradford.** The turn-of-the-century, family-run Bradford has an appealing, old-fashioned feel. An old wooden elevator carries you from the flower-filled lobby to the spacious, comfortable rooms, some equipped with Louis XVI-style furniture, brass beds, and fireplaces. Not all rooms have TV. Some rooms with shower qualify as moderate. *10 rue St-Philippe-du-Roule, 75008, Métro: St-Philippe-du-Roule, tel. 45–63–20–20, fax 45–63–20–07. 36 rooms with bath, 12 with shower, 2 suites with bath. English spoken. Facilities: bar. AE, DC, MC, V.*

Inexpensive
★
Argenson. This friendly, family-run hotel provides what may well be the best value in the swanky 8th arrondissement. Some of the city's greatest sights are just a 10-minute walk away. Old furniture, molded ceilings, and skillful flower arrangements add to the charm. An ongoing room-by-room renovation means new bathrooms in many. The best rooms have full bath, but they are moderately priced; reserve well in advance for one of these. The smallest rooms have shared baths and are inexpensive. *15 rue d'Argenson, 75008, Métro: Miromesnil, tel. 42–65–16–87. 5 rooms with bath, 19 with shower, 3 with shared bath. Some English spoken. DC, MC, V.*

9th Arrondissement (Opéra)

Very Expensive
Grand Hotel Inter-Continental. It's Paris's biggest luxury hotel, with endless hallways and a facade that seems as long as the Louvre. And after four years of thorough restoration this 19th-century gem sparkles like new. The grand salon, with its Art Deco dome, is a registered landmark. All rooms and suites have been luxuriously redecorated in Art Nouveau style. The famed Café de la Paix is one of the city's great people-watching spots. *2 rue Scribe, 75009, Métro: Opéra, tel. 40–07–32–32, fax 42–66–12–51. 470 rooms, 23 suites, all with bath. English spoken. Facilities: 3 restaurants, 2 bars, secretarial services, travel agency, shops, parking. AE, DC, MC, V.*

Moderate
Hôtel du Pré. Located near the pretty square Montholon, slightly off the beaten track, this three-star hotel was thoroughly remodeled in the 1980s. Its reasonable prices, charming and sunny public areas, comfortable rooms done in summery colors, and large bathrooms make it a very good deal. The owners also run the equally good Relais du Pré and Résidence du Pré on the same street (at numbers 16 and 15). *10 rue Pierre-Sémard, 75009, Métro: Poissonière, tel.*

42–81–37–11, fax 40–23–98–28. 22 rooms with bath, 19 with shower. English spoken. Facilities: bar. AE, V.

Inexpensive **Riboutté-Lafayette.** This small, cozy two-star hotel in a 19th-century building near the busy rue La Fayette is family-run and filled with charming bric-a-brac and old furniture. The clean, sunny rooms are decorated in pastel colors, and those on the top floor have sloping ceilings. *5 rue Riboutté, 75009, Métro: Cadet, tel. 47–70–62–36, fax 48–00–91–50. 15 rooms with bath, 9 with shower. English spoken. V.*

11th Arrondissement (Bastille)

Moderate **Méridional.** This three-star hotel in a 19th-century building is a five-minute walk from either the Bastille or the Marais. It's located on a handsome but busy tree-lined boulevard. Though the lobby is a bit garish, the comfortable, quiet rooms are simply decorated in earth tones. The hotel was entirely remodeled in 1991. Prices are lower in winter. *36 blvd. Richard Lenoir, 75011, Métro: Bréguet-Sabin, tel. 48–05–75–00, fax 43–57–42–85. 26 rooms with bath, 10 with shower. English spoken. AE, DC, V.*

Inexpensive **Résidence Alhambra.** This hotel is on the edge of
★ the historical Marais quarter and is conveniently close to five Métro lines. The Alhambra's gleaming white exterior and flower-filled window boxes provide a bright spot in an otherwise drab neighborhood. The smallish guest rooms are painted in fresh pastel shades and have marble-topped breakfast tables. The lobby is filled with plants and leather armchairs. Most rooms have color TV, unusual for hotels in this price range. The reception area and breakfast room were remodeled in 1992. *13 rue de Malte, 75011, Métro: République, tel. 47–00–35–52, fax 43–57–98–75. 10 rooms with bath, 48 with shower. English spoken. MC, V.*

12th Arrondissement (Gare de Lyon)

Moderate **Modern Hôtel-Lyon.** This three-star, family-run hotel, conveniently located between the Bastille and the Gare de Lyon, changed ownership in 1992. As a result, rooms have been remodeled and redecorated in light colors, and many bathrooms are being upgraded. The new owners are as friendly and helpful as their predecessors. *3 rue Parrot, 75012, Métro: Gare de Lyon, tel. 43–43–41–52, fax 43–43–81–16. 36 rooms with bath, 12 with shower. English spoken. Facilities: bar. AE, MC, V.*

13th Arrondissement (Les Gobelins)

Inexpensive **Résidence les Gobelins.** Located five minutes from the Latin Quarter, this simple, small two-star hotel on a quiet street offers pleasant rooms in warm, coordinated colors. The breakfast room faces a small flower-filled garden. There's cable TV in every room. *9 rue des Gobelins, 75013, Métro: Gobelins, tel. 47–07–26–90, fax 43–31–44–05. 18 rooms with bath, 14 with shower. English spoken. AE, DC, MC, V.*

14th Arrondissement (Montparnasse)

Moderate **Royal.** This small hotel, set in a late-19th-centu-
★ ry building on attractive boulevard Raspail, has won much praise, especially from American guests. The mood throughout is stylish yet simple, with salmon-pink rooms and a wood-paneled, marble-floored lobby filled with plants. You can sit in the small conservatory, where drinks are served; there's no bar or restaurant. This hotel is borderline expensive, but worth it. *212 blvd. Raspail, 75014, Métro: Raspail, tel. 43–20–69–20, fax 42–79–95–23. 33 rooms with bath, 15 with shower. English spoken. AE, MC, V.*

Inexpensive **Midi.** This hotel is close to both Montparnasse and the Latin Quarter, and there are Métro and RER stations nearby. Don't be put off by the nondescript facade and reception area; most of the rooms are adequately furnished, and those facing the street are both large and quiet. Request room 32, if possible, and avoid the cheapest rooms, which are quite dingy and unattractive. *4 av. Réné-Coty, 75014, Métro: Denfert-Rochereau, tel. 43–27–23–25, fax 43–21–24–58. 20 rooms with bath, 21 with shower, 9 with shared bath. Some English spoken. No credit cards.*

16th Arrondissement (Trocadéro/Bois de Boulogne)

Moderate   **Queen's Hotel.** One of only a handful of hotels located in the desirable residential district around rue la Fontaine, Queen's is within walking distance of the Seine and the Bois de Boulogne. The hotel is small and functional, but standards of comfort and service are high. Flowers on the facade add an appealing touch. Most rooms with shower are inexpensive. *4 rue Bastien-Lepage, 75016, Métro: Michel-Ange-Auteuil, tel. 42–88–89–85, fax 40–50–67–52. 7 rooms with bath, 15 with shower. English spoken. MC, V.*

18th Arrondissement (Montmartre)

Moderate   **Regyn's Montmartre.** Despite small rooms (all recently renovated), this small, owner-run hotel on Montmartre's place des Abbesses is rapidly gaining an enviable reputation for simple, comfortable accommodations. A predominantly young clientele and a correspondingly relaxed atmosphere have made this an attractive choice for some. Try for one of the rooms on the upper floors, with great views over the city. *18 pl. des Abbesses, 75018, Métro: Abbesses, tel. 42–54–45–21, fax 42–54–45–21. 14 rooms with bath, 8 with shower. English spoken. MC, V.*

Inexpensive   **Utrillo.** Newly renovated, the Utrillo is on a quiet side street at the foot of Montmartre. The decor is appealing, with prints in every room and a marble-topped breakfast table. Because the color white is emphasized throughout, the hotel seems light, clean, and more spacious than it actually is. *7 rue Aristide-Bruant, 75018, Métro: Blanche, tel. 42–58–13–44, fax 42–23–93–88. 5 rooms with bath, 25 with shower. English spoken. Facilities: sauna. AE, DC, MC, V.*

6 The Arts and Nightlife

The Arts

The weekly magazines *Pariscope*, *L'Officiel des Spectacles*, and *7 à Paris* are published every Wednesday and give detailed entertainment listings. The best place to buy tickets is at the venue itself. Half-price tickets for many same-day theater performances are available at the **Kiosque Théâtre** across from 15 place de la Madeleine; expect a line. There's another branch at Châtelet RER station (closed Sun.).

Theater   A number of theaters line the Grands Boulevards between Opéra and République, but there is no Paris equivalent to Broadway or the West End. Shows are mostly in French. **Le Mogador** (25 rue de Mogador, 9e, tel. 42–85–45–30) is one of Paris's most sumptuous theaters. Classical drama is performed at the distinguished **Comédie Française** (Palais-Royal, 1er, tel. 40–15–00–15). You can reserve seats in person about two weeks in advance, or turn up an hour beforehand and wait in line for returned tickets.

A particularly Parisian form of theater is *Café-Théâtre*—a mixture of satirical sketches and variety show riddled with slapstick humor and viewed in a café setting. It's fun if you have a good grasp of French. We suggest either the **Café de la Gare** (41 rue du Temple, 4e, tel. 42–78–52–51) or Montmartre's pricier **Chez Michou** (80 rue des Martyrs, 18e, tel. 46–06–16–04).

Concerts   Before the new Opéra de la Bastille opened, the **Salle Pleyel** (252 rue du Fbg. St-Honoré, 8e, tel. 45–63–07–96), near the Arc de Triomphe, was Paris's principal home of classical music. The Paris Symphony Orchestra and other leading international orchestras still play here regularly. Paris isn't as richly endowed as New York or London when it comes to orchestral music, but the city compensates with a never-ending stream of inexpensive lunchtime and evening concerts in churches.

Opera   The **Opéra** itself, or **Opéra Garnier** (pl. de l'Opéra, 9e, tel. 47–42–53–71) has alas conceded its role as Paris's main opera house to the **Opéra Bastille** (pl. de la Bastille, tel. 40–01–16–16). The old Opéra now devotes itself to classical dance; French ballet superstar Patrick Dupont is the reigning artistic director. The Opéra Bastille, meanwhile, has had its share of start-up and management problems, and many feel it is not living up to its promise of grand opera at affordable prices. In the lofty old hall of the **Opéra Comique** (5 rue Favart, 2e, tel. 42–90–12–20), you'll hear often excellent comic operas and lightweight musical entertainments. The **Théâtre Musical de Paris,** better known as the Théâtre du Châtelet (2 pl. du Châtelet, 1er, tel. 40–28–28–28) offers opera and ballet for a wider audience, at more reasonable prices.

Dance   Apart from the traditional ballets sometimes on the bill at the Opéra (*see above*), the highlights of the Paris dance year are the visits of major foreign troupes, usually to the **Palais des Congrès** at Porte Maillot (tel. 40–68–22–22) or the **Palais des Sports** at the Porte de Versailles (tel. 48–28–40–48).

Movies   There are hundreds of movie theaters in the city, and a number of them, especially in principal tourist areas such as the Champs-Elysées and the boulevard des Italiens near the Opéra, run English films. Check the *Officiel du Spectacle* or *Pariscope* for a movie of your choice. Look for the initials "v.o.," which mean *version originale;* i.e., not subtitled or dubbed. Cinema admission runs from 40 francs to 55 francs; there are reduced rates on Wednesdays and, in some cinemas, for morning shows. Most ushers expect a franc or two tip. Real movie buffs should visit the **Pompidou Center,** with lots of classics and obscure films.

The Champs-Elysées bristles with cinemas, among them the **Pathé Marignan-Concorde** (No. 27), **Gaumont Ambassade** (No. 50), **Gaumont Champs-Elysées** (No. 66), **Publicis** (No. 129), and the **George V** (No. 146). Big-screen fanatics should try the **Max Linder Panorama** (24 blvd. Poissonière, 9e), the **Kinopanorama** (60 av. de la Motte-Piquet, 15e), or the **Grand Rex** (1 blvd. Poissonière, 2e).

On the Left Bank, the Action chain of cinemas, including the **Action Ecoles** (23 rue des Ecoles, 5e), **Action Rive Gauche** (5 rue des Ecoles, 5e), and **Action Christine** (4 rue Christine, 6e), show offbeat films and reruns; so do the **Studio Galande** (42 rue Galande, 5e), the **Saint-André-des-Arts** (30 rue Saint-André-des-Arts, 6e), and the **Lucernaire Forum** (53 rue Nôtre-Dame-des-Champs, 6e). The Chinese-style **Pagoda** (57 rue de Babylone, 7e) is a national monument, and well worth a visit.

Nightlife

The French are definitely nightbirds, though these days that means smart, elegant *bars de nuit* rather than frenetic discos. The **Champs-Elysées,** that ubiquitous cabaret land, is making a comeback, though the clientele remains predominantly foreign. The tawdry **Pigalle** and down-at-the-heels **Bastille** areas are trendy these days, and the **Left Bank** boasts a bit of everything. During the week, people are usually home after closing hours at 2 AM, but weekends mean late-night partying.

Cabaret Paris's nightclubs are household names, shunned by wordly Parisians and beloved of foreign tourists, who flock to the shows. Prices can range from 350 francs (simple admission plus one drink) to more than 1,000 francs (dinner plus show). For 600 francs, you can get a good seat plus half a bottle of champagne.

The **Crazy Horse** (12 av. George V, 8e, tel. 47-23-32-32) is one of the best known clubs for pretty girls and dance routines, lots of humor, and lots less clothes. The **Moulin Rouge** (pl. Blanche, 18e, tel. 46-06-00-19), that old favorite in Montmartre, mingles the can-can and crocodiles in an extravagant spectacle. The **Lido** (116 bis av. des Champs-Elysées, 8e, tel. 40-76-56-10) stars the famous Bluebell Girls and tries to win you over through sheer exuberance. The legendary **Folies Bergères** (32 rue Richer, 9e, tel. 42-46-77-11), expected to reopen by the end of 1993, is still renowned for its glitter.

Bars and Nightclubs The more upscale Paris nightclubs tend to be both expensive (1,000 francs for a bottle of gin or whiskey) and private—in other words, you'll usually need to know someone who's a member in order to get through the door. It helps to be famous to get into **Les Bains** (7 rue du Bourg-l'Abbé, 3e). **Keur Samba** (73 rue La Boétie, 8e) has a jungle setting. The Pigalle area in Montmartre is becoming the place to be nowadays, despite its reputation as a seedy red-light district. Among hot places here are: **Moloko** (26 rue Fontaine, 9e), a smoky late-night bar for all ages; **la Poste** (34 rue Duperré, 9e), with dinner and dancing; **Lili la Tigresse** (98 rue Blanche, 9e), a sexy bar with a trendy crowd; and—not to be missed—the brasserie **Pigalle** (22 blvd. de Clichy, 18e), whose '50s frescoes and ceramics have been classified as a national treasure.

Other popular spots are **Le Rosebud** (11 bis rue Delambre, 14e), a cult spot for the Jeunesse Dorée (young and fashionable) of the Left Bank; **La Casbah** (18 rue de la Forge Royale, 11e), a bit of Casablanca in the Bastille area; and **le Forum** (4 blvd. Malsherbes, 8e), an archtypical French cocktail bar with one of the best selection of drinks in Paris.

Some fun places for an evening out include: **Caveau des Oubliettes.** Listen to Edith Piaf songs in a medieval cellar that was once the dungeon of a prison. It's complete with minstrels, troubadours, and serving wenches—and tourists love it. *11 rue St-Julien-le-Pauvre, 5e. Admission: 130 frs. Open 9 PM–2 AM. Closed Sun.*

Au Lapin Agile. It considers itself the "doyen of cabarets," and Picasso once paid for a meal with one of his paintings. The setting in Montmartre is touristy but picturesque. *22 rue des Saules, 18e. Admission: 110 frs. Open 9 PM–2 AM. Closed Mon.*

La Rôtisserie de l'Abbaye. French, English, and American songs are accompanied by the guitar in a medieval setting. You can dine here, too. *22 rue Jacob, 6e. Admission: 200–350 frs. Open evenings only.*

Madame Arthur. A wacky, burlesque transvestite-and-drag show that's not for the fainthearted. *75 bis rue des Martyrs, 19e. Admission: 280 frs, including show. Open evenings only.*

L'Ane Rouge. A mixed Parisian and foreign crowd frequent this typical French cabaret. The emphasis is on laughs, and entertainment includes singers, magicians, comedians, and ventriloquists. *3 rue Laugier, 17e. Admission starts at 200 frs including show. Open 8 PM–midnight.*

Jazz Clubs The French take jazz seriously, and Paris is one of the great jazz cities of the world, with plenty of variety, including some fine, distinctive local coloring. For nightly schedules, consult the specialty magazines *Jazz Hot* or *Jazz Magazine*. Remember that nothing gets going till 10 or 11 PM, and that entry prices can vary widely from about 35 francs to over 100 francs.

Start on the Left Bank at the **Caveau de la Huchette** (5 rue de la Huchette, 5e), a smoke-filled shrine to the Dixieland beat. **Le Petit Journal** (71 blvd. St-Michel, 5e), opposite the Luxembourg gardens, serves up good food and traditional jazz. **Le Bilboquet** (13 rue Saint-Benoît, 6e) plays mainstream jazz in a faded Belle Epoque decor. Nearby, the **Montana** (28 rue Saint-Benoît, 6e) is a well-known spot for jazz lovers. **La Villa** (29 rue Jacob, 6e), a newcomer on the jazz scene, has been attracting serious musicians.

Elsewhere in the city, **Au Duc des Lombards** (42 rue des Lombards, 1er) is an ill-lit, romantic venue. **Le Petit Opportun** (15 rue des Lavandières-Ste-Opportun, 1er) is a converted bistro that sometimes features top-flight American soloists with French backup. The **Slow Club** (130 rue de Rivoli, 1er) plays swing and Dixieland jazz. **New Morning** (7 rue des Petites Ecuries, 10e) is a premier spot for visiting musicians and French bands. The **Lionel Hampton jazz club** at the Meridien Hotel near Porte Maillot (81 blvd. Gouvion-St-Cyr, 17e) also boasts top jazz artists.

Rock Clubs Most places charge from 80 to 100 francs for entrance and get going around 11 PM. Leading English and American groups usually play at the large **Bercy** or **Zenith** halls in eastern Paris; check posters and papers for details. To hear live rock in a more intimate setting, try the **Dancing Gibus Club** (18 rue du Fbg. du Temple, 11e), a place of long standing. The **Locomotive** (90 blvd. de Clichy, 18e) claims to offer rock's cutting edge, and **Le Bataclan** (50 blvd. Voltaire, 11e) features mostly French punk rock bands. **Le Sunset** (60 rue des Lombards, 1er) is a small, whitewashed cellar with first-rate live music. The legendary **Olympia** (28 blvd. des Capucines, 9e, tel. 47–42–25–49), once favored by Jacques Brel and Edith Piaf, still hosts leading French singers.

Discos The **Balajo** (9 rue de Lappe, 11e), is a Bastille institution that thumps to sounds old and new. On the same street, the **Chapelle des Lombards** (19 rue de Lappe, 11e) goes for an Afro-Cuban beat. Those with a penchant for Latin rhythms should try the **Trottoirs de Buenos-Aires** (37 rue des Lombards, 1er) for some mambo, samba, and salsa. **Le Tango** (13 rue Au-Maire, 4e) attracts a sensuous dance crowd. **La Java** (105 rue du Faubourg du Temple, 11e) still seems hung up on the '60s, while **Club Zed** (2 rue des Anglais, 6e) is a prime rock'n'roll venue for all ages. The famed **Le Palace** (3 cité Bergère, 9e), one of Paris's best-known clubs, has been bought by fabled nightclub owner Régine, who is currently remodeling it. Check to see if it has reopened when you visit.

Pubs The **Académie de la Bière** (88 bis blvd. de Port-Royal, 5e) serves more than 100 foreign brews to accompany good french fries and *moules marinière* (mussels cooked in white wine). The **Bar Belge** (75 av. de Saint-Ouen, 17e) is an authentically noisy Flemish drinking spot, while the **Mayflower** (49 rue Descartes, 5e) is a classy Left Bank spot, British-style. The **Micro-Brasserie** (106 rue de Richelieu, 2e), just off the Grands Boulevards, brews its own beer.

Casinos The nearest public casino, **Casino d'Enghien** (tel. 34–12–90–00), is by the lake at Enghien-les-Bains, 10 miles to the north of Paris.

For Lesbians and Gays **Chez Moune** (54 rue Pigalle, 18e) is a cabaret and disco for lesbians. Upscale **Katmandou** (21 rue du Vieux Colombier, 7e) is Paris's best-known lesbian nightclub. Gay men can try the popular **Le BH** (7 rue du Roule, 1e) or **Broad Connection** (3 rue de la Ferronerie, 1er).

Index

Fodor's Travel Guides

Available at bookstores everywhere, or call 1–800–533–6478, 24 hours a day.

U.S. Guides

Alaska

Arizona

Boston

California

Cape Cod, Martha's Vineyard, Nantucket

The Carolinas & the Georgia Coast

Chicago

Colorado

Florida

Hawaii

Las Vegas, Reno, Tahoe

Los Angeles

Maine, Vermont, New Hampshire

Maui

Miami & the Keys

New England

New Orleans

New York City

Pacific North Coast

Philadelphia & the Pennsylvania Dutch Country

The Rockies

San Diego

San Francisco

Santa Fe, Taos, Albuquerque

Seattle & Vancouver

The South

The U.S. & British Virgin Islands

The Upper Great Lakes Region

USA

Vacations in New York State

Vacations on the Jersey Shore

Virginia & Maryland

Waikiki

Walt Disney World and the Orlando Area

Washington, D.C.

Foreign Guides

Acapulco, Ixtapa, Zihuatanejo

Australia & New Zealand

Austria

The Bahamas

Baja & Mexico's Pacific Coast Resorts

Barbados

Berlin

Bermuda

Brazil

Brittany & Normandy

Budapest

Canada

Cancun, Cozumel, Yucatan Peninsula

Caribbean

China

Costa Rica, Belize, Guatemala

The Czech Republic & Slovakia

Eastern Europe

Egypt

Euro Disney

Europe

Europe's Great Cities

Florence & Tuscany

France

Germany

Great Britain

Greece

The Himalayan Countries

Hong Kong

India

Ireland

Israel

Italy

Japan

Kenya & Tanzania

Korea

London

Madrid & Barcelona

Mexico

Montreal & Quebec City

Morocco

Moscow & St. Petersburg

The Netherlands, Belgium & Luxembourg

New Zealand

Norway

Nova Scotia, Prince Edward Island & New Brunswick

Paris

Portugal

Provence & the Riviera

Rome

Russia & the Baltic Countries

Scandinavia

Scotland

Singapore

South America

Southeast Asia

Spain

Sweden

Switzerland

Thailand

Tokyo

Toronto

Turkey

Vienna & the Danube Valley

Yugoslavia

Special Series

Fodor's Affordables

Caribbean

Europe

Florida

France

Germany

Great Britain

London

Italy

Paris

Fodor's Bed & Breakfast and Country Inns Guides

Canada's Great Country Inns

California

Cottages, B&Bs and Country Inns of England and Wales

Mid-Atlantic Region

New England

The Pacific Northwest

The South

The Southwest

The Upper Great Lakes Region

The West Coast

The Berkeley Guides

California

Central America

Eastern Europe

France

Germany

Great Britain & Ireland

Mexico

Pacific Northwest & Alaska

San Francisco

Fodor's Exploring Guides

Australia

Britain

California

The Caribbean

Florida

France

Germany

Ireland

Italy

London

New York City

Paris

Rome

Singapore & Malaysia

Spain

Thailand

Fodor's Flashmaps

New York

Washington, D.C.

Fodor's Pocket Guides

Bahamas

Barbados

Jamaica

London

New York City

Paris

Puerto Rico

San Francisco

Washington, D.C.

Fodor's Sports

Cycling

Hiking

Running

Sailing

The Insider's Guide to the Best Canadian Skiing

Skiing in the USA & Canada

Fodor's Three-In-Ones (guidebook, language cassette, and phrase book)

France

Germany

Italy

Mexico

Spain

Fodor's Special-Interest Guides

Accessible USA

Cruises and Ports of Call

Euro Disney

Halliday's New England Food Explorer

Healthy Escapes

London Companion

Shadow Traffic's New York Shortcuts and Traffic Tips

Sunday in New York

Walt Disney World and the Orlando Area

Walt Disney World for Adults

Fodor's Touring Guides

Touring Europe

Touring USA: Eastern Edition

Fodor's Vacation Planners

Great American Vacations

National Parks of the East

National Parks of the West

The Wall Street Journal Guides to Business Travel

Europe

International Cities

Pacific Rim

USA & Canada

WHEREVER YOU TRAVEL, *H*ELP IS NEVER FAR AWAY.

From planning your trip to replacing
lost Cards, American Express® Travel Service
Offices* are always there to help.

PARIS

11 Rue Scribe
1-47-777-707

38 Avenue de Wagram
1-42-275-880

5 Rue de Chaillot
1-47-237-215

155 Avenue Victor Hugo
1-47-274-319

83 Bis, Rue de Courcelles
1-47-660-300

Euro Disney®
Disneyland Hotel
Marne la Vallée
1-60-456-520

**American Express Travel Service Offices are found in
central locations throughout Paris.**